AF239838

'[Amish's] writings have generated immense curiosity about India's rich past and culture.'

– Narendra Modi
(Honourable Prime Minister of India)

'[Amish's] writing introduces the youth to ancient value systems while pricking and satisfying their curiosity…'

– Sri Sri Ravi Shankar
(Spiritual Leader and Founder, Art of Living Foundation)

'{Amish's writing is} riveting, absorbing and informative.'

– Amitabh Bachchan
(Actor and Living Legend)

'Amish is one of India's greatest storytellers, creative, imaginative, so you have to turn the page.'

–Lord Jeffrey Archer
(One of the highest-selling authors of all time)

'[Amish's writing is] a fine blend of history and myth … gripping and unputdownable.'

– BBC

'Thoughtful and deep, Amish, more than any author, represents the New India.'

– Vir Sanghvi
(Senior Journalist and Columnist)

'Amish's mythical imagination mines the past and taps into the possibilities of the future. His book series, archetypal and stirring, unfolds the deepest recesses of the soul as well as our collective consciousness.'

– Deepak Chopra
(World-renowned Spiritual Guru and Bestselling Author)

'[Amish is] one of the most original thinkers of his generation.'
— *Arnab Goswami*
(Senior Journalist and MD, Republic TV)

'Amish has a fine eye for detail and a compelling narrative style.'
— *Dr Shashi Tharoor*
(Member of Parliament and Author)

'[Amish has] a deeply thoughtful mind with an unusual, original and fascinating view of the past.'
— *Shekhar Gupta*
(Senior Journalist and Columnist)

'To understand the New India, you need to read Amish.'
— *Swapan Dasgupta*
(Member of Parliament and Senior Journalist)

'Through all of Amish's books flows a current of liberal, progressive ideology: about gender, about caste, about discrimination of any kind… He is the only Indian bestselling writer with true philosophical depth – his books are all backed by tremendous research and deep thought.'
— *Sandipan Deb*
(Senior Journalist and Editorial Director, Swarajya)

'Amish's influence goes beyond his books, his books go beyond literature, his literature is steeped in philosophy, which is anchored in bhakti, which powers his love for India.'
— *Gautam Chikermane*
(Senior Journalist and Author)

'Amish is a literary phenomenon.'

— *Anil Dharker*
(Senior Journalist and Author)

DHARMA

Amish is a 1974-born, IIM (Kolkata)-educated banker-turned-author. The success of his debut book, *The Immortals of Meluha* (Book 1 of the Shiva Trilogy), encouraged him to give up his career in financial services to focus on writing. Besides being an author, he is also an Indian-government diplomat, a host for TV documentaries, and a film producer.

Amish is passionate about history, mythology and philosophy, finding beauty and meaning in all world religions. His books have sold more than six million copies and have been translated into over twenty languages. His Shiva Trilogy is the fastest-selling and his Ram Chandra Series the second fastest-selling book series in Indian publishing history. You can connect with Amish here:

- www.facebook.com/authoramish
- www.instagram.com/authoramish
- www.twitter.com/authoramish

Bhavna Roy was educated in Mussoorie, Pune and Mumbai. After graduating in psychology from Mumbai University, she qualified for the Indian Administrative Services. Having trained partly at the LBSNAA, she quit and then worked first as a volunteer in a school for special children in Malegaon, and then in an NGO in Nashik called SOS. She is the wife of the late Himanshu Roy IPS. She lives in Mumbai.

Celebrating
30 Years of Publishing
in India

Other Titles by Amish

SHIVA TRILOGY

The fastest-selling book series in the history of Indian publishing

The Immortals of Meluha (Book 1 of the Trilogy)

The Secret of the Nagas (Book 2 of the Trilogy)

The Oath of the Vayuputras (Book 3 of the Trilogy)

RAM CHANDRA SERIES

The second fastest-selling book series in the history of Indian publishing

Ram – Scion of Ikshvaku (Book 1 of the Series)

Sita – Warrior of Mithila (Book 2 of the Series)

Raavan – Enemy of Aryavarta (Book 3 of the Series)

War of Lanka (Book 4 of the Series)

INDIC CHRONICLES

Legend of Suheldev

NON-FICTION

Immortal India: Young Country, Timeless Civilisation

AMISH
& BHAVNA ROY

DHARMA

DECODING THE EPICS
FOR A MEANINGFUL LIFE

HarperCollins *Publishers* India

First published in 2020

First published in India by HarperCollins *Publishers* 2022
HarperCollins *Publishers* India, Cyber City, Building 10-A, Gurugram,
Haryana – 122002, India
www.harpercollins.co.in

2 4 6 8 10 9 7 5 3 1

P-ISBN: 978-93-5629-309-0
E-ISBN: 978-93-5629-310-6

Typeset by SÜRYA, New Delhi

HarperCollins *Publishers*, Macken House, 39/40 Mayor Street Upper,
Dublin 1, D01 C9W8, Ireland

To Bhavna's husband & Amish's brother-in-law,
the late Himanshu Roy.

Many speak of noble ideals,
few live them,
and very few inspire those they leave behind
to be better than they are.
Himanshu was one such noble soul.

We try, every day, to follow his path.
We hope that when we meet him again,
we don't disappoint him.

CONTENTS

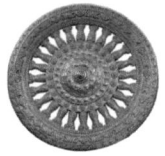

ACKNOWLEDGEMENTS

*The acknowledgements written below were composed when the book was published in 2020. I must also acknowledge those that are publishing this edition of **Dharma**. The team at HarperCollins: Swati, Shabnam, Akriti, Gokul, Vikas, Rahul, Poulomi and Udayan, led by the brilliant Ananth. Looking forward to this new journey with them.*

***

The late Himanshu Roy: husband to Bhavna, brother-in-law to Amish; a guide to both. The late Dr Manoj Vyas: father-in-law to Amish, uncle to Bhavna; a fount of wisdom for both. Their honour, grace and dignity continue to inspire us.

Neel, Amish's young son. My life, my soul. The Covid pandemic raging this year meant that I couldn't travel from London to Mumbai easily, and didn't see him enough. But the skies did open up. And I did see him, and hold him. *Bhagwan ke ghar der hai, andher nahin.*

Anish, Meeta and Ashish, our siblings and sister-in-law, for always being there. Our rocks of Gibraltar.

The rest of our family: Usha, Vinay, Shernaz, Preeti, Donetta, Smita, Anuj, Ruta, Mitansh, Daniel, Aiden, Keya, Anika and Ashna. For their constant faith and love.

Also, Navin, Anu, Nitin, Vishal, Avni, Mayuri, Khushi, Annie, Pia. For being Bhavna's family of the heart.

Sivan and Yaron Barzilay, who are Bhavna's spiritual gurus. In every true sense, the epitome of friends, philosophers and guides.

Gautam, the CEO of our publisher Westland, and Karthika and Deepthi, our editors. This is a very different book, a mix of fiction and non-fiction; their advice, support and guidance played a huge role in bringing this project together. The rest of the marvellous team at Westland: Amrita, Arihant, Arunima, Christina, Divya, Jaisankar, Krishnakumar, Madhu, Mustafa, Naveen, Neha, Nidhi, Raju, Sanghamitra, Sanyog, Sateesh, Satish, Saurabh, Shatrughan, Vipin, and many others. They are the best team in the publishing business.

Aman, Vijay, Shubhangi, Anuj, Padma, Divya, Seema, Sharvika, Chanchal, and the rest of Amish's colleagues at his office in Mumbai. They take care of the business, which gives him enough free time to write.

Mehul, who looks after Bhavna's personal office. He enables her to live a purposeful life.

Gavin Morris, who designed the stunning cover of this book.

Hemal, Neha, Hitesh, Punit, Prakash, Beverly, Harshada and Team OktoBuzz. They have made most of the marketing material for the book and all the digital activities. We have worked with them for many years. One of the best teams in the business.

Mayank, Deepika, Sneha, Naresh, Vishaal, Sarojini, Kirti and the Moe's Art team, who have driven media relations and marketing alliances for the book. Calm and wise in media relations, they are an asset to the team.

Ashish Mankad, a super-talented designer, and more importantly, a thinker, who helps guide and drive the art for Amish's books.

Satya and his team, who have shot the author photos of Amish that have been used on the cover of this book. He made a rather ordinary subject look better.

Neha Jivrajka-Basu for the author photo of Bhavna. And Reshma Aziz for the make-up and outfit for the photo. Their talent outstrips the material they were given.

Preeti, a publishing industry wizard, who works on the international deals for Amish's books.

Sandeep, Caleb, Akhil, Kshitij, and their respective teams, who support Amish's work with their business, legal and marketing advice.

Mrunalini, a Sanskrit scholar, who works with us on research.

Aditya, a passionate reader of Amish's books, who has now become a friend to both Bhavna and Amish, and also a fact-checker.

Brij, Narayan, Archana, Sandeep, Olivier, Ravichandran and Somnath, who are a part of Amish's team at Nehru Centre, London, for their love and support.

Rajinder Ganju, who typeset this book.

And last, but certainly not the least, you, the reader. Your consistent affection, understanding and encouragement is what we deeply cherish. Thank you so much. May Lord Shiva bless all of you.

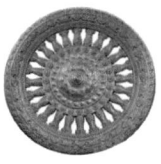

INTRODUCTION

Both of us, brother and sister, had a unique privilege in our upbringing. We were immersed in two worlds.

The first was Bharat, this blessed land whose ancient roots sink deep and from which we seek inspiration. We were raised in a deeply traditional household steeped in our culture, religion (primarily Hinduism, but also Buddhism, Jainism and Sikhism), scriptures and rituals. Our paternal grandfather, Pandit Babulal Sunderlal Tripathi, was a Sanskrit scholar who taught math and physics in Kashi, at the Banaras Hindu University. Our maternal grandmother, Smt. Shankar Devi Mishra, was a teacher in Gwalior and also a scholar of scripture and tradition. The long shadows cast by these two remarkable individuals continue to influence our family. They keep us rooted.

There was also another influence, of India, a land

playing catch up with the world, with modernity and Western-style liberalism, in pursuit of which it often imitated the UK, and later the USA. Our parents were raised in a Hindi-speaking milieu, both at home and in school. And they suffered for it. Lack of proficiency in English was a debilitating limitation in getting good jobs and achieving career progression, especially in an economy laid waste by socialist policies. Our parents decided that their children would not endure what they had. We are four siblings, and we were all packed off to the most elite educational institutions of the time. It was a stretch, since it was way beyond their social and economic means. However, our mother was determined, as she said, to ensure that her children grew up around the *angrezi-waalas*, so that we would not ever be intimidated by them. It was especially important to her that her children succeed in this new world.

Thanks to our education in elite boarding and day schools, we grew up with an insider's view of the anglicised India of the time. It had its strengths. It had its beauty. It certainly had panache. But there was a subtle denigration of the Hindu way of life, which often angered us. We kept quiet though, as our mother had advised us to. She would often quote Lord Krishna to us, and one of the lessons we learnt from the Lord was: 'Pick your battles with wisdom. Fight from a position of strength.' She also exhorted us to recognise that there is something to be learnt from everyone and everything, even from those who denigrate your way of life.

So we learnt to straddle the two worlds. Shakespeare in school, Kalidasa at home. George Bernard Shaw in school, Mahabharata and Ramayana at home. Johann Sebastian Bach in school, Pandit Bhimsen Joshi at home. The Bible in school, the Gita and the Upanishads at home. The Beatles and Lata Mangeshkar, both at school and home! We boisterously lived the Western life in school and fervently practised our rituals at home. Our education prepared us for life in the modern world but taught us almost nothing of our own traditions. These, we learnt at home. From our elders, who kept the flame of our ancient culture alive within us.

India is the only surviving pre-Bronze Age civilisation; we are still vibrantly alive. Every other pre-Bronze Age civilisation is dead, existing only as lifeless shells within the walls of museums and academia today. Our ancestors protected and kept alive that which is most precious: our culture. Often, they did so by fighting off brutal foreign invaders. Most importantly, they passed the flame forward. From generation to generation. In an unbroken chain. We too must pass the torch forward. To the next generation.

We recall reading somewhere: 'Traditions are not the worship of ashes, but the preservation of fire.'

This book is the first of many in which we reflect upon and discuss different facets of Indian culture. Some we can learn from, some we can adapt, and some we must let go of.

We have not followed the usual, modern style of non-fiction books, which are built upon a hypothesis and then backed up with references to support that hypothesis. This style, we believe, leads to adversarial tribalism, even among scholars. This is evident in debates in which scholars often strive to prove loyalty to 'their tribe' and attack those on the opposite side, instead of honestly seeking the truth with an open mind. These debates generate more heat than light.

We have followed the ancient Indian Upanishadic style of conversations which present different views, even contrarian views. We have tried our best to not make the lessons we draw from these prescriptive, only suggestive. For you must make up your own mind.

You might ask, why dharma? Don't we understand the concept by now? But dharma is quite the Scarlet Pimpernel among words. Difficult to pin down, it is invisible to the eye and confounding in the extreme. Shift the definition just a little, and it slides into another meaning. Yet, it is the universe within which Indian philosophy nestles.

Our endeavour in this series of books will be to find and explore multiple strands that lead to the dharmic centre. We have embedded these explorations in a fictional setting, with a repeating cast of characters, each of whom has stories to tell. We hope that over the years, Gargi and Nachiket, Anirban and Valli, Lopamudra and Dharma Raj, and a few others still waiting in the wings, will come alive in your minds, as they have in ours. Perhaps you will identify with one or the other, or several of them, at various stages in your own evolving relationship with the epics and the stories they tell. Our interpretations are also moored to some other, more modern interpretations of these stories. Amish's Meluhan universe flows alongside and intersects the popular version of the Mahabharata today, to together serve as the soil from which we attempt to extract an understanding of ethics, morality, compassion, rigour, restraint, aspiration, wisdom and many other imponderables. The biggest lesson might well be that there are many paths to wisdom, and it is possible for each of us to find our fit without compromising another's.

Lastly, it must be stated with humility that we are not experts. We do not have the brilliance of our babaji and naniji. Indeed, of your babaji or naniji either.

The flame of reflection has grown weaker in our generation. The blessings of Goddess Lakshmi have increased dramatically, but Goddess Saraswati's grace is not as easily bestowed. And yet, this is a sincere effort. We are hoping to pass on a torch to you. Hold it aloft and run with it. And, if you find it worthy, pass it on.

Mother India is special. The only one with an unbroken chain, with roots extending back to the dawn of human civilisation. Let's keep the flame alive. For the more we share it, the more it will grow. And all of us can benefit from ancient India's light.

अपूर्वो कोऽपि कोशोऽयं विद्यते तव भारति ।
व्ययतो वृद्धिमायाति क्षयमायाति सञ्चयात् ।।

(Apoorvah kopi koshoyam vidyate tav Bharati,
Vyayato vruddhim aayaati kshyam aayaati sanchayaat.)

My Goddess Saraswati, your treasure is unique,
It grows when spent and reduces when hoarded.

Note: Sources referred to in the main body of the text, which is structured as conversations among a fictional group of characters, are listed in the Select Bibliography at the end of the book.

1

WHAT IS KARMA ANYWAY?

Nachiket grabbed the keys from the mantelpiece with one hand as he stuffed his mouth with the remains of an omelette sandwich with the other. His work bag almost knocked over a flower vase, which was placed on the console near the entrance. Gargi shrieked. Steadying the vase, Nachiket yanked open the door.

'Visit Baba on your way back. You haven't seen him for five days now,' said Gargi.

'Okay. Bye.'

He glanced at his watch as he ran down the stairs. Ten minutes to nine. *I won't make it. Lord Shiva help me!*

He jumped on his bike and revved the engine. Almost skidding on a loose tile, he spun onto the road. *I'm gonna be roasted.*

Nachiket Anant Sawant was a sous-chef. He worked at the oddly named Hotel Ego in Shivaji Nagar. He lived in Baner, not too far from the hotel. But Pune traffic was usually insane.

Shockingly, the road was free. He steadied his breath

and settled into a comfortable ride. Within minutes, he was at the hotel. He parked his bike in the compound at the back. 9.10 a.m. *Phew.*

Good karma!

It was seven in the evening when Nachiket turned onto the leafy Prabhat Road. His hand flew reflexively to his chest as he passed the Ganesh temple on the side of the road. He turned into the second lane on the right and slowed as he reached the last bungalow at the end of the lane. He brought the bike to a halt in front of the rickety wooden gate. Getting off, he pushed open the gate, straightening the nameplate on the side before going through. *Dharma Raj Deshpande.* Nachiket smiled to himself as he parked the bike under the neem tree and stepped onto the veranda.

'Ketu? *Aalas ka, baala?* Is that you, child?'

Nachiket halted at the main door and turned his head toward the beloved voice of his father-in-law. The old man sat on a swing at the far end of the veranda. Nachiket walked up to him.

'*Namaskar karto,* Baba.' Nachiket touched his feet, then sank into a cane chair, a sigh of exhaustion escaping his lips.

'Tough day?' Baba's voice was soft.

'Hmmm ... Karma!'

'Karma, is it? How so?'

Nachiket was nonplussed. 'I don't know. I just said it!'

'Hmmm. Okay.' Dharma Raj took off his reading glasses and leaned back, rubbing his nose.

Nachiket's eyes fell on the book in Dharma Raj's hand. *Raavan: Enemy of Aryavarta*. 'Gargi is reading that same book. And I finished it just last week. Is that why you are thinking of karma today? What exactly is karma anyway? What was Raavan's karma?'

Dharma Raj: 'Very impactful, evidently. It's been a while and we're still talking about him!'

Nachiket laughed.

Dharma Raj: 'What do you think? What was his karma? Was he a victim or was his life a consequence of karma?'

'Both, maybe?'

Dharma Raj sat back, one arm stretched over the cushions at the back. 'Hmmm ... How tired are you?'

'Why?'

'I was thinking ... How serious an answer do you want?'

Nachiket sat up straight. His tiredness dissipated like magic. *We are going to talk. Yes!*

Baba read his mind. 'Go ask Aai for two cups of tea. If possible, some bhajis. Let's fix the setting first!'

As Nachiket rose, Dharma Raj quipped, 'And, if you can manage it, her exalted presence too!'

Nachiket laughed as he walked indoors to greet his mother-in-law.

Minutes later, he walked back and settled down on the floor cushion under the window. At his guru's feet. 'Tell me, Baba. What is karma?'

'What does it mean to you?' Dharma Raj countered.

'Good begets good. Bad begets bad,' Nachiket said. 'Although that does seem like I am stating the obvious.'

His father-in-law frowned. 'Don't be flippant. What is good? What is bad? Huh?'

Nachiket shrugged. 'You tell me.'

'Karma is activity. Action. To do.'

'Good and bad action, both?'

Dharma Raj was silent, as if thinking about what to say next. But Nachiket knew better.

'All right, Ketu, tell me. Was Liu Xiaobo a good man? Of good karma?'

For a moment, Nachiket was thrown. What did the Chinese dissident have to do with karma, good or bad?

He said, 'I don't know. But thank God he got the Nobel Prize before he died. The man spent his life in prison for his principles, his convictions ...' His voice trailed away.

Dharma Raj smiled. 'All he wanted to do was to rid his country of the Communist Party of China, the CPC.'

'Yes!' Nachiket exclaimed.

Dharma Raj: 'Do you know that the CPC has raised more than 630 million people out of poverty in the last thirty years? How much of an impact has Liu Xiaobo had on the world, in real terms? Or even on the Chinese people?'

Nachiket: 'So, what you are saying is, Xiaobo may not be "good" and the CPC may not actually be "bad"?'

Dharma Raj: 'The CPC is a political party driven by one purpose only: to seek power and remain in power. In this case, over the Chinese nation.'

'Sometimes it seems like the CPC wants to rule the entire world!' Nachiket ventured. 'So, judging by intentions, Xiaobo's karma is good. However, by outcome, the CPC's karma is better because it pulled so many Chinese people out of poverty. But what about Dr Li Wenliang then, the whistleblower? Or this Wuhan coronavirus for that matter, which the CPC has unleashed on the world, causing hundreds of thousands of deaths and massive economic destruction? They've pretty much wiped out their good karma points, I'd say!'

Dharma Raj continued as if he had not heard him, 'So many organisations are more about sustaining themselves than eradicating a problem or achieving a goal. Anti-addiction centres, women's support organisations ... Ever noticed that? Not all NGOs, not the ones I admire! But many. It appears that anti-poverty and climate change efforts are best conducted at conferences these days. The fancier the location, the more sincere the effort!'

Nachiket smiled. He enjoyed his Baba's dry wit. Sardonic, but never cynical. He could make you laugh at yourself without ever mocking you. He said, 'Baba, you didn't answer my question about Dr Li Wenliang. Or the coronavirus.'

'I don't want to. It will take us towards sociopolitics, and I wouldn't want to do that in the absence of our wives. Leave world politics for another day.'

'Okay.'

Dharma Raj: 'Speaking of ineffective organisations, some of the best people I know are the do-nothing-talk-amazing types. The wonderful tribe of fence sitters! Beginning with me! And, mind you, some fence sitters have a particular penchant for passing judgments! How long does one wait to evaluate outcomes, anyway?'

Nachiket: 'I'm really confused now. How does one judge?'

Dharma Raj tossed his first challenge. 'Why judge? Why not just understand?'

Nachiket: 'But how?'

Dharma Raj: 'By understanding karma's relationship with dharma.'

Nachiket: 'Woah ... it's the deep end now!'

Dharma Raj: 'What do you mean?'

Dharma Raj was a retired police officer. A celebrated officer with a reputation for toughness and large-heartedness. Nachiket often felt as if he was being tested by him. And he was never sure whether he had failed or passed.

'I don't know, Baba,' he said now. 'I don't know what I mean. Tell me. What is dharma?'

Dharma Raj: 'Have you heard of Icarus?'

Nachiket: 'Yes. James Bond. *Die Another Day.*'

Dharma Raj: '*Na re!* No, no! Let me tell you a story. An old story.'

Nachiket: 'From ancient India?'

Dharma Raj: 'No. Ancient Greece.'

'All right.' Nachiket leaned back against the wall. He loved listening to Baba's stories.

King Minos rules the island of Crete, which is separated from Athens by the Sea of Crete. One day, the king secretly summons the famous craftsman Daedalus to his court. Daedalus comes to his palace in the dead of night. Minos asks him to build a complex maze, which would be a prison for the Minotaur, a monster that is half man and half bull.

Daedalus completes the task to the king's satisfaction, and names his creation the Labyrinth. Minos wants to hide it from his wise daughter Ariadne. But Daedalus reveals the secret to her. This angers Minos, and he imprisons Daedalus in the Labyrinth, along with his young son Icarus.

Daedalus knows his way out of the maze. After all, he built it. But he also knows that the king will have them killed the moment they emerge from it.

Daedalus is a master craftsman. He fashions two sets of wings from wax and feathers; one pair for himself and one for his son.

The father warns the son as he fastens his wings, 'My son, do not fly with less energy, for you will fly too low, and the damp waters of the sea will leaden your wings. But do not fly with too much energy either. If you get too close to the sun, the wax on your wings will melt. Heed me, child, and follow my path.'

He has cautioned Icarus against both complacence and hubris. But Icarus is young and vibrant. Alive! He flies toward the sun, lost in exultation. Soon, the wings are gone, and he falls like a stone into the sea and drowns, his hands still flapping in wonder. Millennia later, it still carries his name: Icarian Sea.

Nachiket wondered aloud, 'Why was the king secretive? He was the king, na? Who was he afraid of? Seems to me, the wise daughter had a very unwise father. Ungrateful, too. Poor Daedalus.'

'What about Icarus? Don't you feel sorry for him?' Dharma Raj asked sardonically.

Nachiket shrugged. 'Him too ... But I'm distracting you. What's the moral of the story?'

Dharma Raj: 'Forget morals. Dharma is more interesting than that!'

Nachiket tilted his head expectantly. 'Okay, so where does dharma come into the picture here?'

'It's quite simple, really. Dharma is that which holds and sustains. All life—not just human life—has an ideal expression; a best state. When a living thing is in a state of dharma, it is the way it was meant to be. The sun, the moon, the stars ... They are sustained. They hold.'

Nachiket: 'You call that simple? I'm stumped. What do you mean by the best state?'

Dharma Raj: 'Let me put it this way. A diamond may be said to have achieved its dharma because the carbon molecules that constitute it have reorganised themselves in the best possible order. On the other hand, the molecules of coal may be seen as struggling with their karma. Coal is useful, but it's a work in progress. Given time—a very, very long time—a diamond may be born. The banyan tree has attained its dharma; the simple weed struggles with its karma. Who knows, one day, it may bear fruit!'

Nachiket: 'Dharma sounds very elusive, going by all that you've said so far.'

Dharma Raj: 'It's also multifaceted, and I am only touching upon one facet. You cannot translate this word into any other language. Call it the natural order, the cosmic law ... When you find your purpose and rhythm in the universe, you are in a state of dharma. Even a lion on the hunt is in a state of dharma. And the hunted deer too.'

Nachiket: 'Baba, tell me that story again. It's the one Vedavati tells Raavan, isn't it?' His eyes drifted to the book on the table beside Dharma Raj.

'Yes. So, this is what happens. In a jungle near the river port of Amaravati, an ageing lion struggles to feed his cubs. They are starving; he is starving. Then he spots a doe with her fawns in the grassland. One of them is weak, the runt of the family. On spotting the lion, the mother alerts her children, and they flee towards the treeline. But the runt is trailing. The lion—well past his prime—charges towards the weakling and begins to close the distance between himself and the tiny fawn. And then, something magnificent happens. The mother slows her pace, offering herself as a sacrifice until her little one can manage to get ahead. Soon she comes to a complete stop and stands still, watching her children move towards safety. The lion also halts, confused. He looks at the doe, one short leap away. He looks at the fawns, safely at a distance now and bleating for their mother. He turns and looks at his own children, emaciated and hungry ... Should he kill the doe to feed his children? Or should he give her the gift of life?'

Nachiket: 'What do you think happened next?'

Dharma Raj: 'It doesn't matter. Either way, it's a conundrum without a clear solution.'

Nachiket said thoughtfully, 'Baba, when Vedavati tells Raavan this story, she is speaking to him of dharma, isn't she?'

Vedavati is the Kanyakumari, the virgin Goddess. According to a tradition of veneration in many parts of India, the Mother Goddess resides temporarily in the body of certain chosen girls. These girls are worshipped as living Goddesses. People flock to them for advice and prophecies; even kings and queens do. Till they reach puberty, at which point, it is believed, the spirit of the Goddess moves into the body of another pre-pubescent girl.

Ancient India is dotted with Kanyakumari temples. The Kanyakumari in *Raavan: Enemy of Aryavarta* is from Vaidyanath, in eastern India. Once, on the way home from Amarnath in Kashmir, her entourage stops at Rishi Vishrava's ashram by the river Yamuna, a stone's throw away from Indraprastha. She speaks to no one, but there is an aura about her, a kind of magnetism. Even Raavan is bewitched.

Raavan is the precocious firstborn of Vishrava, the distinguished rishi. He is four years old when he first meets his *Dhruv tara*, his *North Star*: Vedavati. At age seven, already showing signs of a fearsome intellect, he starts training in the martial arts, the fine arts and the material sciences. He becomes an accomplished veena player, especially skilled with the Rudra veena. He is also a closet sadist. Arrogant, manipulative, harsh. And yet, deeply vulnerable to the Kanyakumari.

When she tells him, 'You can be better', for a heartbeat, he contemplates the possibility. Then the feeling dissolves in an onslaught of anger.

Dharma Raj: 'Yes. Vedavati represents dharma; she is dharma. But tell me why you said that. Give me an example.'

Nachiket: 'Okay. Remember the time Raavan tied up a rabbit to do that macabre experiment of his? The excitement was building inside him, his heart was beating rapidly ... and then he sensed her presence. He looked up and the Kanyakumari was just standing there. Tranquil. Expressionless. She untied the rabbit, kissed it on the forehead and let it bound away. And Raavan was immobile. Transfixed!'

Dharma Raj: 'Even the rabbit became quiet in her hands. Harmony resonates and transmits if you allow it to. As for Raavan, I don't know if he was transfixed or just for one moment: fixed! Like the lion in the story.'

Nachiket: 'So, if every living creature must aspire to be the best they can, would you say the planets in our universe are also in a state of dharma? The way they unfailingly revolve around the sun ...'

Dharma Raj: 'Yes. And the sun follows its dharma, its assigned role in the Milky Way.'

Nachiket: 'And what is the dharma of the universe? Or is it the multiverse?'

Dharma Raj: 'Perhaps that's beyond our understanding. But these celestial bodies have achieved a rhythm over billions of years. We must assume that they are in the state they were always meant to be in.'

Nachiket: 'I suppose for lesser, out-of-balance beings like us, the dharmic state is out of reach for now. Hmmm?'

'Hmmm ...' Dharma Raj nodded in agreement.

Nachiket: 'I'm reminded of the Chinese Tao of Lao Tzu.'

Dharma Raj: 'You're right. Tao means "the way", "the path". The Chinese believe that the Tao is the source of cosmic order. It keeps the universe in rhythm and balance.'

Nachiket: 'You know my friend Anirban?'

Dharma Raj: 'Anirban Kothapalli. The Telugu man who married a Thai woman.'

Nachiket: 'Yes. His wife's name is Malivalaya. We call her Valli. Valli told us about the state of *wei wu wei:* doing without doing. Apparently, Lao Tzu said that anyone who realises the Tao is in a state of *wei wu wei,* even if it lasts for a fleeting moment. It's effortless action, when the doer and the doing become one. Deliberate effort disappears when that happens. The doer becomes a tool of nature.'

Dharma Raj: 'So, when Lata Mangeshkar sang *Tere sur aur mere geet*, she was in *wei wu wei*.'

Nachiket: 'M.S. Subbulakshmi. "*Kaatrinile varum geetham*". Dharma.'

Dharma Raj: 'Maria Callas singing a flawless soprano!'

Nachiket: 'Nadia Comăneci on the balance beam!'

Dharma Raj: 'Sufi dervishes whirling in a trance!'

Nachiket: 'So, dharma lies in a state of naturalness?'

Dharma Raj: 'Be careful. You young people love the idea of being your "natural self". There are two types of naturalness, you know. One has to do with our animal nature. It's instinctive, without awareness. Unexamined and childlike. We're all creatures of habit, and habits are mechanical.'

Nachiket smiled. 'Some habits are useful, though. I don't get up in the morning and consciously decide which hand to use while brushing.'

Dharma Raj: 'You have a point. Imagine wondering which leg to first pull your trousers over. But most habits are limiting. Especially the emotional patterns one falls into.'

Nachiket: 'Like your daughter's habit of taking offense. Being critical.'

Dharma Raj drew in a sharp breath. 'Or yours, of indulging pain! The drama, the mood spins—classic Devdas!'

'You're biased, Baba!' Nachiket complained.

'Are you objecting to the bias or the direction of the bias?'

'Oh, stop it, you two! You know he's right about your precious daughter, Raj.'

They turned as a voice rang out from behind them. Nachiket's mother-in-law walked up to him and handed him a cup of tea. She handed another cup to her husband and settled into the cane chair beside him with her favourite masalo, milk flavoured with saffron, grated dry fruit and jaggery.

Dharma Raj: '*Yaa, yaa*, Guruji, *basaa*; come, sit.'

Lopamudra cast her husband an enigmatic look. 'Continue, wise guy.'

2

SWADHARMA VS DHARMA

Nachiket often thought that Lopamudra and Dharma Raj had achieved the essence of togetherness. Two strong individuals, their marriage had evolved from volatile beginnings to a respectful calm, and finally, an easy companionship. In the first decade of their life, she talked. In the second decade, he talked. Thereafter, they both listened. They had earned each other's ear. Dharma Raj called their marriage a *pairidaeza*, a Persian walled garden, the root of the word paradise. She said the garden had a few rough patches.

Dharma Raj placed his cup on the tray with slow deliberation. 'I'm talking about another kind of naturalness: cosmic, not human. For instance, the sun, the planets and the stars are natural entities. The way the plants on earth respond to the sun and the rain is natural. This naturalness is like a symphony. Predictable but complex, like an intricate, interconnected pattern. *Indra jaal. Indra's net.* None of the elements are unconnected. They work in tandem.'

Lord Indra weaves a magical net and spreads it across the vast expanse of nothingness. It has no beginning and no end. It just goes on and on and on ... expanding without cessation. The net is connected by nodes, each node a dazzling jewel of throbbing potential as well as a reflection of every other jewel. The jewels are linked by lines of energy, sometimes called *bandhu. Kinship. Relation.*

No jewel is allowed an independent existence, and they are continually replaced by their progeny. Nothing exists outside this weave. It is the *Indra jaal. Indra's net.* Within it, everything is a reflection of everything else. Microcosms within the expanding, evolving macrocosm of life.

The *Indra jaal* is mentioned in the Atharva Veda, and also in the Buddhist Avatamsaka Sutra. The Japanese call it *Kegon.* It is a stunning metaphor for cosmic interpenetration and interdependence.

Nachiket: 'Anirban was talking about cell memory the other day. That cells carry not only physiological data but also emotional and praanic energy data down the generations. He thinks that modern science is finally colliding with mysticism!'

Dharma Raj: 'He's right. Cells carry strong emotional data from very early in life—when you are only a few days old, perhaps. What I felt when my mother screamed at me, or someone around me, when I was a one-year-old, that feeling is strongly imprinted in my physiology to this day. Confucius said, "What you see, you remember." Your cells remember what you saw, even from a time when you had not learned a single word to express it in. By the way, this friend of yours seems to be interesting, I must say. The academic sort. You must bring him over one day.'

Nachiket: 'Sure. He would love that. He's an internationalist kind of guy. A travelling Indian. But tell me, even if not all of us, are there at least a few who can lay claim to this higher naturalness?'

Dharma Raj: 'If they lay claim to it, they don't have it! A few have achieved this higher naturalness. Very few. Lord Ram. Lord Shiva. Lord Ganesh. Zarathustra. Mahavir. Gautam Buddha. Jesus Christ. Guru Nanak. But most of us are so set in our ways that our habits become our identity. Like people often say these days, "This is what I am. Take it or leave it".'

Nachiket: 'Then what is the difference between us and the animal world?'

Lopamudra: 'Not much! You give a dog a bone, it's happy. You take away the bone, it's unhappy. You cannot educate a dog to be unhappy when the bone is given, or happy when the bone is taken away—Baba's words.'

Dharma Raj smiled.

Nachiket: 'But with a human being, that is a possibility, na?'

Dharma Raj: 'Yes, a possibility. But remember, we're part animal. It's built into our evolutionary biology. We have a reptilian brain. We must ask ourselves: What is this bone we have been given? What or who is our controller?'

Nachiket: 'It seems so obvious! Why is it so difficult then?'

Dharma Raj: 'Because our ego blocks the way. Which brings us to the tool of karma.'

Nachiket: 'And we're back to the start! So, what is karma?'

Dharma Raj: 'Karma, like I said, is activity; to do. And activity should be a tool for self-discovery. You have to walk that path alone, though. Understand your own inner drama. Confront it. Then master it. That will bring you closer to dharma.'

Nachiket: 'I'm lost.'

Dharma Raj: 'Daedalus is dharma, that which stays the course. *Aapan sagale Icarus aahot. We are all Icarus.* We engage with karma and work towards our best state. Remember one thing. We are engaged in activity every minute of our life.'

Nachiket: 'Even when we are asleep?'

Dharma Raj: 'Yes. Activity is movement. So, even the thoughts that run through our mind, consciously or unconsciously, comprise activity. Dreams are activities. Every time a thought enters my mind, or an emotion tugs at my heart, it's a form of action.'

Nachiket: 'Even breathing is action then.'

Dharma Raj: 'Of course! Strong action.'

Nachiket: 'Why strong? The best breathing is smooth and easy, isn't it?'

Lopamudra: 'The way we breathe is fundamentally linked to our well-being. Breath and emotions are inextricably connected. We can control our emotions with our breathing. And with a better grip on our emotions, we can change the way we think and behave. Which is why breathing can be described as strong and impactful action.'

Dharma Raj: 'Getting back to where we were, an activity can be dull and repetitive: Icarus flying too low. Or it can be energetic. But even that can lead us astray: Icarus flying too high. If our actions are motivated by fear, passion, anxiety, desire—if they are driven by the ego—then even hard work can take us away from dharma. Only balance is sustainable. When action is neither less nor too much.'

Nachiket: 'How do we know what is balanced? How do we know we are good or bad?'

Dharma Raj: '*Arre*! You're back to good and bad!'

Lopamudra: 'Were the Pandavas good and the Kauravas bad?'

Nachiket's eyes flew to his mother-in-law. She had spoken softly. Holding her cup close to her lips, she said, 'You want to understand dharma and karma? Start with Gandhari.'

Subala is the king of Gandhara, modern-day Kandahar in Afghanistan. He has one daughter, Gandhari. The youngest among his sons is the scheming master-gambler Shakuni. Astrologers had foretold that Princess Gandhari's first husband would die young. Fearing for her, Subala gets his girl-child married to a goat, which is sacrificed after the wedding ceremony. Technically, Gandhari is now a child widow.

Years later, she is married to the elder son of the Kuru household, Dhritarashtra. When brought to her marital home in Hastinapura, she discovers that her husband was born blind. She then decides to blindfold herself for life. Does she do it to spite the Gods? Is it anger? Rage? Frustration? Or her moral fibre on display? The preferred narrative is of the Great Sacrifice.

Nachiket: 'Why Gandhari?'

Lopamudra: 'Okay then, Bhishma, the other Great Sacrificer. Sacrifice is a good place to start examining the ego. We may cover other nooks and corners and even graduate to Arjuna tonight!'

Nachiket: 'Are we going to tell stories now?'

Lopamudra: 'These are stories only on the surface. Go deeper and you touch wisdom.'

Dharma Raj: 'I'm okay with the surface. Let me say that upfront. War. Ambition. Love. Hate. Schemes. Machinations. Wrongs. Rights ... *Kya baat hai*! Fantastic!'

Nachiket: 'We'll leave the surface for when Gargi is with us.'

Dharma Raj: 'You think my daughter is shallow?'

'I think your daughter loves stories. Your daughter is my wife, Baba,' Nachiket said wryly.

Lopamudra shook her head, her eyes gleaming with mischief. 'All his philosophy flies out of the window in a second. Aristotle with a lollipop. Go below the surface, Raj!'

Dharma Raj raised his eyebrows. 'There was a time when I was your lollipop, Madam Aristotle!'

Lopamudra: 'You still are—mine!'

Dharma Raj: 'If you say so!'

Nachiket broke the moment. 'So, what lies below the

surface, Aai? I know what Anirban would have said:
"Lift the veil of Isis!"'

Lopamudra: 'Isis?'

Isis is the wife of Osiris, the ruler of the Egyptian
Gods. They rule the heavens, and everything is
perfect at first. But, as often happens, there is a
scheming brother. His name is Seth. He wishes to rid
himself of his brother and replace him. It is difficult,
though, for Osiris is a good ruler, and his wife is the
Goddess of wisdom and love.

Seth throws a party and tricks Osiris into playfully
entering a sarcophagus. As soon as Osiris lies down,
Seth snaps the coffin shut and flings it into the river
Nile. He then declares himself king of the Gods.

Isis will not accept this fate. She sets off down the
Nile in search of her husband. After a series of trials
and tribulations, the determined wife locates the
coffin entangled in a tree. She finds her Osiris.

On being informed of this by the crows, his spies,
Seth rushes to the spot and chops Osiris into fourteen
pieces before he can be revived by his wife. He
scatters the pieces all over Khem, Ancient Egypt. Isis
does not give up. She travels the length and breadth
of the kingdom, retrieving the pieces. She finds them

all, except his genitals, and manages to revive him. But he is infertile now. And so Osiris becomes the guardian of the land of eternity.

Sometime later, Isis magically bears a child, and the couple name him Horus. Horus fights Seth, but neither can win. Finally, the wounded uncle and nephew declare a truce. Horus is declared king of the earth.

Dharma Raj: 'The Isis of antiquity. She is the Egyptian Goddess of wisdom. Also, the dancing Goddess. Lopa, you remember the dance on that ship in Cairo? On the Nile? The veil of Isis. She reveals the secret of life as each veil lifts. Beyond all the veils is the complex world of karma.'

Nachiket: 'Hmmm ... But to get back to the Indian tale ... Aai?'

Lopamudra: 'I love these Egyptian stories. Nachiket, don't think of the characters of the Mahabharata, or any epic, as people. Think of them as qualities: our virtues and vices. The battle of Kurukshetra is staged within us, every day, every moment. And, like Baba says, don't judge, only understand.'

Nachiket: 'But they're all so vivid! So real!'

Lopamudra: '*Tari suddha. Even then.* Spirituality is about the internal world. Think in terms of "me", not "them".'

Nachiket: 'Okay. Help me understand.'

The Mahabharata is the story of the family of Krishna Dwaipayana. We know him as Veda Vyasa, the narrator of the epic. At the heart of the story is the house of Kuru, which rules the kingdom of Hastinapura. It has a glorious heritage of an ancient line of kings, extending back to the great king Bharat, after whom our ancient civilisation is named.

The bloodline of the royal house is threatened with extinction when Devavrata, Shantanu and Ganga's son, takes the *Bhishma pratijna, the terrible oath,* of celibacy. He does this to allow his infatuated father to marry Satyavati, the daughter of the chief of fishermen.

Satyavati and Shantanu have two sons: Chitrangada and Vichitravirya. Chitrangada dies young, and Vichitravirya marries Ambika and Ambalika. But he also dies before fathering any children. And so the Kuru bloodline ends.

But Satyavati has a son, Krishna Dwaipayana, from an earlier encounter with Rishi Parashara. On his mother's request, he impregnates Ambika and Ambalika. Ambika has Dhritarashtra, who is born blind. Ambalika gives birth to Pandu.

Dhritarashtra marries the pious Gandhari, who wilfully blindfolds herself for life. Pandu is made king because of the elder brother's disability.

On being cursed by the sage Kindama, Pandu forsakes the throne and becomes a hermit. He lives in the Satasringa forest with his two wives, Kunti and Madri. Pandu is celibate now, but Kunti has an ace up her sleeve. Many years ago, she had been granted a boon by Rishi Durvasa, that she could have a child by invoking any God she wanted. Using this formula, Kunti gives birth to Yudhishtra, Bhima and Arjuna. She shares the formula with Madri, who gives birth to Nakula and Sahadeva. Together, they are the five Pandavas.

Meanwhile, after an atypical two-year pregnancy, Gandhari gives birth to a cold, fleshy mass. Veda Vyasa asks her to make a hundred pieces of it and store each in a pot of ghee. A year later, they will transform into a hundred sons. Gandhari asks to be allowed to make a hundred and one pieces. She also wants a daughter. Thus are born the Kauravas, the most famous among them being Duryodhana and Dushasana. The only daughter is named Dushala.

Lopamudra: 'The house of Kuru was based in the city of Hastinapura, right? *Hasti* is *elephant* in Sanskrit. And elephants are a symbol of wisdom. So Hastinapura, the city of elephants, is also the city of wisdom.'

Nachiket: 'I am with you ... so far.'

Lopamudra: 'The kingdom is being pulled apart by the rivalry of the cousins. On one side are a hundred brothers. So many! On the other side is the band of five. Now, let your imagination loose. What can this symbolise?'

Nachiket: 'Hmmm ... the internal world ... So, if I'm Hastinapura, then the numerous brothers are my desires, fears, anxieties, denials, ambitions, rationalisations ... my inner Kauravas. They pull me in different directions every day. And the other five are ... my five senses? Are they my Pandavas?'

Lopamudra: 'Not bad! The way I look at it, our senses are raceways that set up the pattern of our Kurukshetra: the ground on which we battle these cousins and brothers. Is one side good and the other evil? That's simplistic. The "evil" Kauravas have their strengths too; the "good" Pandavas have their weaknesses.'

Dharma Raj: 'Wisdom does not invest in simplicity.'

Lopamudra: 'Nice. I'll add that to my list of quotes by you! Anyway, the seeds of so-called evil lie in the failure of goodness. Or injury to goodness. When character devolves, we often find excuses for it, don't we?'

Nachiket: 'When it's our character, yes. Or the character of people we like. Not those we dislike. They are just plain bad, or so we choose to believe!' Nachiket laughed.

Lopamudra: 'When it's our own character under scrutiny, the excuses become justifications. We refuse to accept responsibility. Often, we don't even admit that there is a problem, even to ourselves. We make up stories instead of examining our own selves.'

Dharma Raj: 'On the other hand, good emerges when we battle our inner weaknesses and issues. It's not easy being good, you know. Even for the bravest.'

Nachiket: 'It would not be so difficult if we were honest with ourselves.'

Lopamudra: 'But we're not honest with ourselves, Ketu. It's easier to deceive and give ourselves false comfort. We believe what it suits us to believe. Karma can often challenge and misguide. Like in the case of Gandhari.'

Dharma Raj: 'Gandhari is the ultimate wife, Lopa. What a sacrifice she made!'

Nachiket: 'She blindfolded herself for life. That is quite a sacrifice.'

Lopamudra: 'And sacrifice is a wonderful thing, isn't it? Just like Devavrata's sacrifice.'

King Shantanu falls in love with the river Goddess, Ganga. She agrees to marry him after he promises to never question her actions. Ganga gives birth to seven children. One by one, she drowns each of them in the river. Shantanu cannot contain himself when his eighth son is born. He begs his wife to let him live. Goddess Ganga regretfully reveals her secret to her husband: that these eight Vasus were cursed by Maharishi Vashishtha, and they needed to be killed in this manner, to release them from the curse. She spares the life of this child, Devavrata, but warns that he will lead a tortured life. Also, since Shantanu has broken his promise, she will have to end their marriage.

Devavrata grows up to be an accomplished warrior and an able administrator. The apple of his father's eye, he is also adored by the people of Hastinapura, who wait expectantly for him to become king. But it is not to be. For Shantanu falls in love again. This time, it is Satyavati, daughter of the chief of fishermen. The chief has a condition before he will consent to give his daughter as bride to the old king: that Devavrata will not be king. Ever. That it will be Satyavati's son who ascends the throne after Shantanu. Devavrata then takes the *Bhishma pratijna* to renounce his inheritance and remain celibate; no future progeny of his will compete with those of his stepmother. Thereafter, he is known as Bhishma.

Lopamudra: 'Bhishma—the one who made the Great Sacrifice.'

Nachiket: 'It was admirable; a selfless sacrifice.'

Lopamudra: 'I am sorry, I would call it a self-filled sacrifice. Gandhari's sacrifice is a blind sacrifice. Literally. And Bhishma's sacrifice is self-indulgent.'

Nachiket: 'How?'

Lopamudra: 'Bhishma was aware that he would make an able ruler, husband and father. Yet, he decided to make the Great Sacrifice for the sake of his old father. Shantanu had lived a full life. He should have stepped aside for his capable son.'

Nachiket: 'Shouldn't children respect their elders?'

Lopamudra: 'Of course they should! Please respect your elders. But not every whim and desire of theirs. Elders should also make themselves worthy of respect. A worthwhile street is a two-way street. Individual to individual, our commitment must be from the best in us to the best in the other. We are not duty-bound to cater to the base nature in others, even if they are our parents or teachers.'

Dharma Raj: 'You're right, Lopa. Bhishma did not challenge his father to be his best—or even better. Instead, he catered to Shantanu's basest instincts. He should have told Satyavati's father that he was being unfair. His own swadharma was to be a good king. He should have accepted that.'

Nachiket: 'But why did he do what he did?'

Lopamudra: 'He misunderstood the dharma of a son. Also, he probably had a burning desire to be "great". That is self-indulgence, not sacrifice. It is morally arrogant.'

Nachiket: 'So then, Gandhari's sacrifice is similar. Pointless.'

Lopamudra: 'Absolutely. Pointless and irresponsible. She "sacrificed" by becoming willingly blind. To what? Her husband's weakness. Her son's overarching envy and hubris. She failed both as a wife and a mother. Her actions were adharmic. Without any inner integrity.'

Dharma Raj: 'Strong words.'

Lopamudra: 'Well, she should have seen the truth and translated it for a husband who couldn't see. She should have guided her sons. Instead, she hid her irresponsibility behind the Great Sacrifice. I heard Gargi use an interesting term the other day. Virtue signalling. Totally applies to dear Gandhari!'

Nachiket: 'Reminds me of Sati and Parvateshwar in the Shiva trilogy that we have all read and enjoyed so much.'

Sati is an accomplished warrior and an expert charioteer. Aristocratic. Grave. Honourable. She is a flawless beauty, the picture of grace and dignity. She is honest but detached, always wearing a stoic, faraway look. She lives by the Meluhan code of conduct.

Sati is the princess of Meluha and daughter of King Daksha and Queen Veerini. Unbeknownst to her, she has a twin sister, Kali, who was disowned by her parents at birth. Daksha cunningly bypassed the vikarma law by abandoning his physically deformed baby girl.

The vikarma law is applied to those who suffer adversities in this birth as punishment for the sins of their previous birth. They live with dignity, forbearance and denial, the only way to wipe their karma clean. Both vikarma men and women have their separate orders of penance. 'Who decides that the vikarma have sinned in their previous birth?' Shiva asks Nandi, a Meluhan soldier. He responds, 'Their own karma.' Why would a man fall ill, Nandi wonders, unless he had it coming? Unless the universe was penalising him for the sins of his previous life? This sounds unfair to Shiva, who is a foreigner and does not know the Meluhan ways.

Sati's first child is stillborn (or so she is told). She is declared a vikarma and genuinely believes that she deserves the punishment. Shiva wants to save her, but how do you save a woman who does not want to be saved?

General Parvateshwar is the chief of the Meluhan armed forces. A disciplined warrior, he is uncompromisingly righteous. He is the only high official in Meluha who is not taken in by the arrival of Shiva, the prophesied saviour of beleaguered Meluha. Parvateshwar places his faith in merit and the prowess of his soldiers and citizenry. He does not believe Meluha needs outside help. He is a proud inheritor of the greatest civilisation ever. He is law-abiding. Law-venerating, in fact. He fights his enemies, even if they are unethical, in accordance with the traditional rules of war.

When Shiva wants to marry Sati, Parvateshwar cannot condone it. Sati is his god-daughter, and he will do anything for her. Except break the law.

He does come around to respecting, even worshipping Shiva later in the story, but only after Shiva has earned his respect through his good karma and noble behaviour.

Nachiket: 'Aai, they are your two favourite characters from Meluha, aren't they? Sati and Parvateshwar …'

Lopamudra looked surprised. 'Explain, Nachiket,' she murmured.

Nachiket: 'Let's start with Sati. She sacrificed her life, her goals, her potential, her immense merit … all for the vikarma law. Imagine if Shiva had not come into her life. What would it have amounted to? Aren't we all supposed to work towards realising our potential? She could have chosen to try and change the law. But she needed Shiva to bring her in line with her best self.'

Dharma Raj: 'Lady Sati was saved by Lord Shiva, while a similar temperament in Gandhari met Dhritarashtra's inertia, with unfortunate consequences. Had Lord Shiva not entered her life, the impact of Lady Sati's actions on Lord Ganesh, her son, would have left him on the path of continuous conflict, leading inexorably towards full-blown vengeance. Like it happened with Duryodhana. Gandhari did not exercise any positive control over her son's impulses. His thirst for vengeance led to his destruction.'

Lopamudra: 'And Parvateshwar …?'

Parvateshwar is sworn to celibacy, the result of a series of events that occurred long ago and emanated from the laws of Meluha. In fact, a gradual degeneration of the laws over hundreds of years.

More than a thousand years ago, Lord Ram came to the conclusion that only a society based on merit could be stable. He believed that a person's caste should be determined only by his karma and his abilities, not birth. So he created a practical system to ensure this. All children born in Meluha were compulsorily adopted by the empire. A great city called Maika was built deep in the south, just north of the Narmada river. Pregnant women travelled to Maika for their delivery. They were the only ones who were allowed into the city. The babies were kept back in Maika, and the mothers travelled home. After some time, the child was enrolled in the Meluha Gurukul, a massive school built adjacent to Maika. Every child received the same basic education, with all the resources of the empire made available to him or her. Then, at fifteen, they took a comprehensive exam. The results decided the caste of the child.

At sixteen, the children were offered to applicant parents who belonged to the same caste. The child then moved into the home of the adoptee parents.

This was the original design.

Alas, an exception was made around three hundred years ago. Noble families voted for the husbands and parents of noblewomen to be allowed entry into Maika. Then, fifty years later, there was a further relaxation. The noble families were allowed to keep their birth-children. Only one man opposed this change. Lord Satyadhwaj, Parvateshwar's grandfather. The law was unfair as it broke a basic tenet established by Lord Ram: every law must apply equally to all, without exception. He swore that his family, and their adoptive descendants, would henceforth not have birth-children. Parvateshwar honoured that promise all his life.

Shiva wonders, if the birth law was changed, why not the vikarma law? A Meluhan friend, Brahaspati, tells him, 'There aren't enough noble families affected by the vikarma law.'

Nachiket: 'Both Bhishma and Parvateshwar were dedicated to their kingdom and their vows of celibacy. But, dare I say, Parvateshwar's sacrifice was also coloured by self-indulgence. Ultimately, both chose to stand against dharma. And, ironically, both knew that they were opposing someone they worshipped as a God. Bhishma stood against Krishna and ended up fighting on the side of a person he himself believed was in the wrong: Duryodhana. Similarly, Parvateshwar stood against Shiva and ended up fighting on the side of the person he believed was wrong: Daksha. Why is it that, sometimes, honourable men like Parvateshwar and Bhishma consciously choose to end up on the side that is against dharma?'

Dharma Raj: 'It could be that their previous sacrifices made them morally arrogant. They were so devoted to their vows that they were blind to the fact that these vows were leading them away from dharma and against the larger good. What are the choices available to us when our vows are pitted against dharma itself? If we must choose between our personal morality and the good of others, what must we do?'

Lopamudra: 'What about swadharma? Without Judas, there would have been no Jesus. Judas performed his swadharma too. Not that I am comparing Parvateshwar with Judas, mind you!'

Dharma Raj: 'It would be interesting if you did. The difference lies in the ideas of honour and dishonour. Swadharma cannot be misaligned with honour. It isn't honourable action so much as the honourable roots of action.'

Lopamudra smiled. 'Your favourite word. Bona fides.'

Dharma Raj smiled back at her. 'Swadharma cannot be in misalignment with dharma, the law of life. Then it becomes self-indulgence in the garb of swadharma. Dharma is always a movement towards balance. If swadharma is at odds with dharma, can it be anything but self-indulgence or imagined swadharma?'

Nachiket: 'That is a fine distinction, but I think I get it. Aren't Raavan's actions a product of self-indulgence and not swadharma? Had he taken Vedavati's advice, he could have followed his dharma. But then, without Raavan, there would be no Ram!'

Lopamudra: 'Raavan was driven by his ego. But not Parvateshwar. Or Lady Sati. Also, when Baba says balance, he's talking about internal balance. Not just external. And we're discussing sacrifice.'

Dharma Raj: 'Okay, then let us discuss the unsung Kunti. Boring, huh? But quite the epitome of stoic forbearance and sacrifice.'

Lopamudra: 'Before we get to that, let me also say that both Parvateshwar and Lady Sati are softened by the power of love. Softening needs love. And love needs a beloved. Lady Sati embraces Lord Shiva's love *before* he repeals the vikarma law. And Parvateshwar's magnetic, helpless attraction for Anandmayi is just ... so beautiful.'

Dharma Raj: 'Love pulls them away from being relentlessly tough on themselves, yes. They learn to love themselves in the bargain. Love is immersive. You begin to also see yourself through the eyes of your lover. But back to Kunti now.'

Mathura is a flourishing city on the banks of the Yamuna river. It is ruled by a council of the Yadav clan. One of the members, Surasena, has a daughter called Pritha. His cousin, Kuntibhoja, adopts the quiet girl and renames her Kunti.

One day, Rishi Durvasa, who is known to be ill-tempered, visits the court of Kuntibhoja. He is looked after by the diligent Kunti. Pleased with the young girl, Durvasa grants her a boon: she can summon any God she pleases, whenever she wants, to magically give birth to a child. Kunti's curiosity gets the better of her, and she invokes the sun God, Surya, to test her new ability. The radiant Surya appears and makes her misguided test run successful. A son is born, with golden earrings attached to his ears and a gold armour stitched on to his chest. He is beautiful but doomed.

Frightened, Kunti abandons her newborn child. She places him in a basket and sets him adrift on the Yamuna. The baby is found by Adhiratha, the charioteer of the Kuru clan. He adopts the child and names him Radheya: son of Radha, his childless wife. We know him as the peerless warrior Karna.

On growing up, Kunti chooses Pandu, the prince of Hastinapura, as her husband, in a swayamvar. A few years later, her husband also marries Madri, sister of the king of Madra. As it happens, in the years to come, Kunti will again invoke the gift of Rishi Durvasa, both for herself and Madri. Together, they will give birth to the five Pandavas.

After the death of Pandu and Madri in the forest, Kunti returns to Hastinapura with her five sons. Now begins her endless saga of hardships. The rest of her life is about duty, sacrifice and responsibility. But there is no drama. No self-pity. Her sacrifices are not grand. She protects her children but makes them strong. She does not discriminate between her stepsons and her sons. She quietly ensures that her sons fulfil their destiny.

Nachiket: 'What are the words you would use to describe Kunti?'

Lopamudra: 'Self-sacrificing. Dutiful. Responsible.'

Nachiket: 'Tiring words.'

Dharma Raj: 'They're not tiring at all, if you understand them properly. Sacrificing, for instance, does not mean giving up what you want from life to fulfil someone else's desires and needs. Ask yourself: Why should I sacrifice? For whom? And most importantly, what should I sacrifice? Do I sacrifice my own enlightened self-interest?'

Lopamudra: 'Kunti did her best to challenge her children. To coax them to constantly improve and realise their swadharma. She did not make herself the centre of their world. Many parents succumb to this insecurity. The greatest gift a mother can give her children is to not make herself the centre of their life.'

Nachiket: 'Hmmm ... so, genuine sacrifice is the ability to set aside one's desires and do one's duty?'

Dharma Raj: 'Yes. You must imprison the voice of your inner child when needed, for it can be irresponsible. Ask yourself: can I willingly stay in a state of confinement when I could be doing something else?'

Nachiket: 'But what is the meaning of sacrifice then? Like you said, it cannot be about giving up our own enlightened self-interest.'

Dharma Raj: 'Do not sacrifice your swadharma for anybody's sake. It would not even be in the interest of the person for whom you are misguidedly making that sacrifice. It would merely be mollycoddling. I "sacrifice" to become central to another person's life. That is manipulation, not sacrifice. Instead, we must have the strength to sacrifice the voice of our ego.'

Lopamudra: 'But first, understand your swadharma. Like Lord Ram. Be noble. A sacrifice must be made mindfully. Remember, what is in the interest of the beehive is always in the interest of the bee. The opposite is not always true. Kunti was responsible and assertive. She did what was right. She did not tolerate what was wrong.'

Dharma Raj: 'Excellent point. We need not always bear injustice with fortitude. Or tolerate the bad behaviour of unreasonable people. Our society respects tradition, and there are many who believe we should give in to the needs of others, especially our elders. Or to those in authority. That it is our duty to do so. In reality, though, such actions could be grossly irresponsible. Because by giving in to them, you may be cheating those people of an opportunity to grow and to introspect. You prevent them from examining their own conduct.'

Nachiket: 'What about Ram leaving the palace for the forest when his father and stepmother ask him to? Would you call that a self-indulgent sacrifice? After all, like Bhishma, he too knew he would make a great king someday.'

Dharma Raj: 'Are you referring to Amish's *Ram: Scion of Ikshavaku* or the original Valmiki Ramayana?'

Nachiket: 'The former.'

Ram and Lakshman accompany Maharishi Vishwamitra to Mithila. Ram discovers that the inscrutable maharishi has brought him there for Sita's swayamvar. Sita, the prime minister of Mithila, is the daughter of the philosophical king Janak. Propriety demands that he accede to the decision of his guru. Ram wins her hand and marries her.

Raavan, the king of Lanka, has been insulted by Vishwamitra, and prevented from participating in the swayamvar. He is livid. He mobilises his ten-thousand-strong bodyguard corps beyond the second wall of Mithila and the lake-moat, in the clearing ahead of the forest line.

Vishwamitra proposes the use of *Asuraastra*, a *daivi astra*. But Lord Rudra had banned the use of *daivi astras* many centuries ago, as Sita reminds the sage. They cannot be used without the authorisation of the Vayuputras, Lord Rudra's tribe that resides in Pariha, far beyond the western borders of ancient India. Breaking the law is punishable with banishment for fourteen years. Sita is vehemently against the proposal. She would rather fight Raavan's hordes with her police force. However, the Mithilans are vastly outnumbered and ill-prepared. Ram, Sita and Lakshman put up a valiant show, but they know it is a losing battle.

Vishwamitra subtly corners Ram. 'Your wife's life is at stake. Will you not take a sin upon your soul for the good of others?' Ram fires the *Asuraastra* on Raavan's forces. Mithila is saved, but actions have consequences. And the noble Ram readily embraces his punishment.

Later, he informs his bewildered father, Dashrath, of his decision to banish himself from the Sapt Sindhu for fourteen years, to atone for the sin of firing a *daivi astra* without permission from the Vayuputras. The scheming Kaikeyi's wishes segue into his desire to exile himself, much to Dashrath's dismay.

Lopamudra: 'Lord Ram was clear that he must face the consequences after firing the *Asuraastra*. He insisted that his father punish him. Dashrath did not want to, despite Kaikeyi plonking herself in the *kopa bhavan*. Also, remember, he did not demur at the prospect of returning after fourteen years and accepting the crown. He did not shun it in perpetuity, like Bhishma did.'

Nachiket: 'That's true. It's very different from what Bhishma did.'

Dharma Raj placed a hand on the cushion beside him and heaved himself off the swing. 'Give me a moment.

I'll just be back.' He walked indoors and returned with a book in his hands. He sat down and leafed through the book, then began to read aloud in a voice that had retained its youthful baritone.

'"Are you insane?" shouted Dashrath.

'The emperor was in his new private office in Kaushalya's palace. Ram had just informed Dashrath about his decision to banish himself from the Sapt Sindhu to atone for the sin of firing a *daivi astra* without the permission of the Vayuputras; a decision that had not gone down too well with Dashrath, to say the least.'

Dharma Raj set the book aside. 'This was before Kaikeyi blindsided him by lodging herself in the *house of anger*. In fact, Kaikeyi forced Dashrath's hand by recalling her two boons because the king was hell-bent on disregarding Lord Ram's wish and announcing his son's ascension to the throne the next day.'

Nachiket: 'Ram, meanwhile, had decided to disobey his father outright if he declared him heir apparent. He planned to abdicate the throne and install Bharat as king instead. After which, he would leave for the forest. But that would have meant publicly dishonouring his father's wish, which is why he was relieved when Guru Vashishtha informed him about his stepmother's move.'

Dharma Raj: 'As for blindly obeying people, remember when Guru Vishwamitra sent Lord Ram and Lakshman, along with Arishtanemi, to destroy the Asuras of the old code?'

Maharishi Vishwamitra, chief of the Malayaputras, visits Dashrath, king of Ayodhya. Dashrath is pensive, wondering what the great warrior-sage wants from him. Vishwamitra is famous for his bad temper and impatience.

It turns out that Vishwamitra wants Ram and Lakshman to accompany him on a journey. One of his ashrams is under attack, and he needs the two brothers to defend his abode. Dashrath nervously agrees to send his sons. They sail down the Sarayu river to Vishwamitra's ashram on the banks of the Ganga. Vishwamitra asks the brothers to find the attackers and destroy them. He tells them that the attackers are Asuras of the old code, who will not attack Ayodhyans because Shukracharya, the guru of the Asurans, was from Ayodhya.

The Asura horde is led by Tadaka, the wife of their deceased chieftain, Sumali. Tadaka, Ram discovers, maintains a militia of fifteen soldiers led by her son, Subahu. *Fifteen.* The entire settlement is not more

than fifty people. Ram is bemused. But Vishwamitra
wants them all killed.

Ram confronts the comic, bumbling heroism of the
band at the outskirts of the settlement. After easily
overpowering them, the brothers ride into the crudely
fortified habitat of the Asuras. There, they confront
amateurish battle tactics. Ram subdues them with
his brilliant archery. When they surrender their arms
on realising that the attackers are Ayodhyans, Ram
expresses the desire to speak with them in private.

They tell him that they are following their laws by
repeatedly attacking the Devas and rishis. Maharishi
Shukracharya had enjoined them to bring all,
especially the Devas, to the path of their true God,
Ekam. Ram then convinces them of their errant ways.
He makes them see that they need new laws. He
convinces them to seek refuge in Pariha, where most
Asuras live under the protection of the Vayuputras. He
also convinces the confounded Vishwamitra to help
them find refuge with the Vayuputras.

Dharma Raj held the book slightly open, using his
thumb as a bookmark.

'Lord Ram had clearly committed himself to
following his guru's order. He said to Vishwamitra, "I

will follow your orders, Guruji, because that is what my father has asked me to do." He said that. And yet, when confronted by Tadaka and Subahu's incompetent, foolhardy heroism, he refused to kill them. Instead, he transformed them and even convinced Vishwamitra to send them to Pariha. So much for obedience!'

Lopamudra: 'Responsible people do their rightful duty. You don't need to endure what is wrong and then label it as responsibility or duty. If you insist on buying into this delusion, you will avoid the real responsibilities that come your way.'

Nachiket: 'It's like saying, "I've been responsible long enough. I'm tired now. It's time other people took up the burden."'

Dharma Raj: 'Yes. That is disguised weakness and an inability to assert yourself. You do not need to be subservient to another human being. By indulging his father's infatuation, Bhishma not only tolerated what was wrong—although he, of course, did not see it as wrong—but also elevated himself to greatness. He debased his father's karma as well as his own. He should have stood up to his father.'

Nachiket: 'You're right. It's wrong to willingly submit to adharma. It's certainly not a sign of greatness.'

Dharma Raj: 'A slim but significant line divides right conduct from empty righteousness.'

Nachiket: 'That's an awesome thought, Baba. But how do we know what is rightful duty and what is not?'

Dharma Raj: 'It cannot be taught. It can only be experienced. But I'll give you a clue. Real responsibility and sacrifice bring joy and satisfaction.'

Lopamudra: 'Well said, Raj. If your child, parent, husband, wife or anyone you love is unwell and you look after them, that's being responsible. No fancy meal or exotic holiday could match the joy Baba felt when Gargi did well in an exam with his guidance. Remember the time your head chef made your kotambir wadi the signature dish of your restaurant, Ketu? What a high that must have been. Would you trade it for the pleasure of watching fifty Bollywood movies?'

Dharma Raj: 'Rightful duty is empowering, not debilitating. Lopa, what happened to the bhajjis?'

Lopamudra: 'No bhajjis. But there's khichdi for dinner.'

Nachiket: 'I should be leaving.'

Lopamudra: 'Why don't you stay? I'll call Gargi and ask her to join us for dinner.'

Lopamudra got up and walked briskly away without waiting for a reply.

3

THE BURDEN OF ENVY

Nachiket turned to Dharma Raj. 'Baba, what do you make of Duryodhana?'

Dharma Raj: 'What do *you* make of him?'

Nachiket: 'I don't know. He has always troubled me. His character is not so cut and dried, na?'

Duryodhana, eldest son of a blind father and a blindfolded mother, is born to the sound of wailing dogs in the palace of Hastinapura. It is an ill omen, warns his uncle Vidur. He is born on the same day as Bhima, the cousin who eventually kills him.

Duryodhana is a bundle of contradictions. He is generous and protective, and large-hearted when he wants to be. Once, Drona, the guru of the Kauravas and the Pandavas, organises a contest to display the skills of his students. When Karna expresses his desire to compete, the Pandavas object. He is the son of a charioteer and not a Kshatriya, they say. In truth, they are afraid that the accomplished warrior will upstage Arjuna. Duryodhana then declares Karna the king of Anga, instantly raising his stature. Karna does not forget this gesture and remains a loyal friend to the end of his days.

Duryodhana is a family man. He is respectful to his parents, a loving husband to his wife, Bhanumati, and a protective father to his children. As the eldest brother, he probably earns more respect from his younger siblings than Yudhishtra, the eldest among the Pandavas, from his. His brother Dushasana is devoted to him.

But Duryodhana has reasons to feel cheated in life. Yes, he wants the throne. He is, after all, the firstborn son of his father, who is older to Pandu, the father of the Pandavas. Is it improper to covet what is his, according to law?

Later, Duryodhana wants to marry Subhadra, but she chooses Arjuna. Duryodhana's son Lakshman wants to marry Balarama's daughter, Vatsala. But she chooses Abhimanyu, Arjuna's son. Duryodhana forbids his daughter Lakshmani from marrying Krishna's son, Samba. But she does.

He feels humiliated.

He has his redeeming qualities, but his faults are corrosive. He spirals into hubris, anger, resentment, arrogance, selfishness. And most overpoweringly, envy.

Dharma Raj: 'You're right. It's not so cut and dried.'

Nachiket: 'He felt cheated. It was all a bit unfair.'

Dharma Raj: 'But that's the thing about envy. You find justifications. Envy covers itself with many excuses: it's unfair; I deserve it; she doesn't deserve it; I worked hard for it; he doesn't value it; I was denied the opportunity ...'

Nachiket: 'Some of that may even be true.'

Dharma Raj: 'Perhaps. You may be certain that you deserve what someone else has got. But envy of that sort will only corrode your character. It's your loss. And your choice.'

Nachiket: 'So, envy is the cross that Duryodhana bears?'

Dharma Raj: 'Among others ...'

Nachiket: 'Like?'

Dharma Raj: 'Resentment. They're related, the two. Duryodhana's stand-out vice is envy. Resentful envy. All of us have experienced it at some point in our lives. The interplay between *wanting* and *having*. Sometimes you *have*—a lot—and yet, you are full of toxic resentment. The past lives on inside you, much after its expiry date. And perhaps life has been extremely unfair to you. Like it was to Manthara.'

Manthara is a hard-nosed, brilliant businesswoman, successful even in the anti-mercantile atmosphere of the Sapt Sindhu. A close confidante of the powerful queen Kaikeyi, she is rumoured to be wealthier than the king. It is also whispered that she is close to the demon-king, Raavan of Lanka. Manthara is scheming and manipulative. But she is also wretched.

A childhood encounter with smallpox left her face scarred for life. At age eleven, polio had partially paralysed her right foot, giving her an odd limp. As if that wasn't enough, when she was twenty, she slipped and fell from the balcony of a friend's house. It left her back bent and disfigured. Teased and disdained all her life, she pursues power and influence, and enjoys spreading dread to get back at the world.

Dharma Raj: 'Manthara suffered endlessly. Despite that, she was doing all right as a businesswoman. Or rather, not doing too badly. Then came the last straw. The pride of her life, her daughter Roshni, was brutally raped and murdered. Worse, Lord Ram was determined to not execute Dhenuka, the youngest among the men who were accused of the crime, because he was underage. The law was clear: minors could not be executed. This caused Manthara to become unhinged. She sank into a cesspool of resentment against all and sundry. She had nothing now. She was empty.'

Nachiket: 'How does her story connect with the interplay you mentioned earlier, between *wanting* and *having*?'

Dharma Raj: 'You'll understand it better if we bring Bhima and his elder brother, Hanuman, into the discussion. But do not forget Aai's injunction. *You* are Duryodhana. *You* are Bhima. You are also Manthara. And Hanuman. They are all within you.'

Nachiket: 'Okay.'

Dharma Raj: 'My inner Duryodhana's envy can be destroyed by the strength of Bhima and Hanuman within me. My inner Manthara's resentment, tough as it sounds, can be harnessed by the contentment of Bhima, the self-control of Hanuman; potentially, at least.'

Nachiket: 'Except, it's not so ...'

'Easy? No, it isn't. Our inner Kauravas are compulsive. The Pandava qualities are built with a great deal of hard work—if at all,' Lopamudra said, as she walked back towards the men.

Dharma Raj: 'Have you been listening?'

Lopamudra: 'I've learned the art of listening from you. After a lifetime of interrupting!'

Dharma Raj: 'Well, then, don't interrupt while I'm interrupting, madam!'

Bhima is conceived when Kunti invokes Vayu, the God of wind. Vayu is also the father of mighty Hanuman, and Bhima is the strongest among men. But uncontrolled strength can be exploited by others. This happens with the child Bhima, the bully who enjoys pushing the Kauravas around. One day, they decide to hit back. They poison him, tie him up, and throw him into a river. But the Nagas from the kingdom of Vasuki, the Naga king, come to his rescue.

Physical strength needs to be harnessed and humbled. Bhima's overconfidence is brought down a peg by his elder brother, Vayuputra Hanuman. One day, while the Pandavas are living in exile in the forest, the wind carries a golden-coloured lotus to them. Draupadi is delighted. She asks Bhima to follow the fragrance and bring her some more flowers. Bhima immediately sets off, scrupulously following the sweet smell. As he enters a banana grove, he comes across an old monkey lying in his path.

Bhima commands the monkey to move aside. The aged creature begs him to move his tail out of his way and carry on. Bhima tries to sweep it aside with one hand. It does not move. Surprised, he sets his mace aside and uses both his hands. But the tail does not budge. He stands up and stares at the extraordinary monkey. And suddenly knows that this is his elder brother, Hanuman. Bhima has just received a lesson in humility.

Dharma Raj: 'Unfettered strength is disruptive and purposeless. It can also be exploited. It arouses envy, after all.'

Lopamudra: 'And resentment.'

Dharma Raj: 'People hit back at you. The Kauravas poisoned Bhima and threw him into the river when he bullied them once too often. Had the Nagas not rescued him, he would have died.'

Lopamudra: 'The Nagas, or serpents, have long symbolised attention and awareness in our culture.'

Nachiket: 'Actually, across cultures. Anirban told me about the Mexican God Quetzalcoatl: a feathered snake. He represented wisdom and focus for the Aztecs.'

Lopamudra: 'Quetzalcoatl! A mouthful. Anyway, back to Bhima. He faced hardships, disciplining and repeated attacks before he found the mental focus to use his strength purposefully. Lord Hanuman exercised better control over his strength, and there was no arrogance for him to overcome. Remember the time he fought the tiger, when little Sita and Radhika were visiting him? Of course, this is Lord Hanuman from Amish's Ram Chandra Series, and not the Mahabharat.'

Nachiket: 'Hanu Bhaiya!'

At the age of eight, Sita is sent to Rishi Shwetaketu's gurukul. There, she meets and makes friends with Radhika. 'The universe has conspired to make me your best friend,' Radhika tells her. Indeed it has, for Radhika introduces Sita to her cousin Hanu Bhaiya.

Radhika is the daughter of Varun Ratnakar, chief of a village that is located along the river Shon. Varun has a cousin, Vayu Kesari, whose son is Hanuman. Varun and Vayu Kesari are Valmikis, the tribe left behind by Lady Mohini, the wife of the previous Mahadev, Lord Rudra.

Lord Hanuman frequently travels to Pariha, the magical land that was home to Lord Rudra. He is instantly drawn to Sita and adopts her as his little sister.

Lopamudra: 'Yes. Hanu Bhaiya. His curved knife was designed in such a way that in the hands of a less skilful person, the slightest loss of control could cause the thrusting hand to slip forward along the blade, causing serious injury to the knife-wielder himself. I was riveted by that encounter. It was much more than a fight.'

Radhika and Sita sneak out of the gurukul and walk deep into the forest for their rendezvous with Hanu Bhaiya. Hanuman has arrived laden with gifts for his sisters: a delicate necklace for Radhika and an *ekmukhi Rudraaksh* for Sita. Sita is thrilled. The *teardrop of Rudra* is very difficult to find and is priceless for her, for she is a devotee of Lord Rudra.

But their happy meeting is rudely disrupted by a ferocious tiger. Hanuman senses the danger and gets the two girls to hide safely behind him. He draws out his *khukuri*, a *curved knife*, as the tiger walks into the open, having been denied the element of surprise. Hanuman waits for the attack.

The tiger goes up on its hind legs and extends its front legs, intending to grab the massively built Hanuman, topple him, and pin him to the ground with its claws. Hanuman remains on his feet and holds the tiger by its throat, even as it claws his back. With his right hand, he thrusts the *khukuri* into its stomach, ripping out its intestines and pushing the creature to the ground. The knife has sliced through the tiger's backbone.

Hanuman could have kept still, held his position, and avoided further injury to himself from the tiger's claws till it weakened. But the animal is in agony. Its hind legs are locked in paralysis. Hanuman bends close while the tiger's claws dig deep into his shoulders. He thrusts his blade into the tiger's heart and ends its suffering.

Lopamudra: 'He ripped out the tiger's intestines and pushed the creature to the ground. So far so good. It was a display of sheer strength. But then came self-control and compassion. Even respect. He did not allow the tiger to suffer, but killed it swiftly, despite the agony of the tiger's claws digging deeper into his back because of that action. His own injuries were deep and took months to heal. But his respect for his foe came through. And kindness. Such a person cannot know envy and resentment, which are based on disrespect.'

Nachiket: 'Hanuman also had great respect for Sursa, even though she propositioned him shamelessly. Calling her "madam", "madam", as he reminded her of his celibacy and the inappropriateness of her advances! Always respectful. Never arrogant.'

Dharma Raj: 'Remember one thing: Your strength being under your control, or not, has nothing to do with others or the way they feel about you. Either way, you will attract the envy of the envious. The difference lies in your response.'

Nachiket: 'Baba, you said people who are contented are less likely to be envious.'

Dharma Raj: 'It's true. The secret behind being satisfied lies in understanding the subtle difference between *wanting* and *having*. Most of us think that once we get what we want, we will be happy. Instead, the minute we satisfy one want, another replaces it. We desire something intensely only till we own it. On getting it, we plateau for a bit, and then start wanting the next thing.'

Nachiket: 'Ha! Forgive me, Baba, but I must say this. Gargi's wardrobe is stuffed with forgotten bags, shoes, clothes and *hazaar* other stuff that she once compulsively wanted.'

'Your bathroom is also filled with toiletries and deodorants that you once wanted, Ketu,' Lopamudra gently chided her son-in-law.

Dharma Raj nodded with satisfaction. 'Last month, you got a raise at work. Are you done with wanting further increases in your salary?'

Nachiket: 'But what's so wrong about that? Or, for that matter, with the clothes, shoes and bags? And deodorants too? I'm not eyeing other people's deodorants!'

Lopamudra: 'It's perfectly all right, Ketu. Relax. You don't have to be a sadhu. *Having* is not a problem.

Pleasure is not a problem either. Just keep one thing in mind: pleasure does not last.'

Dharma Raj: 'She's right. *Having* is not a problem at all. It is the never-ending *wanting* that drives us insane. Are you still delighted with the last deodorant you bought? Do you even remember its name?'

Lopamudra: 'Buy another one, tomorrow morning. Just don't let it become an overriding need. It should be equally all right if you never buy a deodorant for the rest of your life. Equanimity is what one strives for.'

Nachiket: 'We're not monks. That kind of contentment would make us lazy and inactive. Passive.'

Lopamudra: 'Yes, there's always that danger. It is difficult to be dynamic, active, comfortable in your own skin and satisfied with what you have, all at the same time. But there *are* such people. And they do what must be done, without getting distracted. They don't wait for someone else to do it for them.'

Nachiket: 'There's something else. When you are not the jealous or envious sort, you take every opportunity to say good things about others. I've always admired the ability to praise ... Not gratuitously, but in an honest way. Spontaneous appreciation, not at all contrived. Gargi is capable of that.'

Dharma Raj: 'So you admire Gargi.'

Nachiket: 'Baba, I've chosen to spend my life with

her! Yes, she is volatile. Hugely opinionated. Aggressive. But precious. A WYSIWYG.'

Dharma Raj: 'What?'

Nachiket: 'What You See Is What You Get! Is she coming over, Aai?'

Lopamudra: 'Of course. But let's get Duryodhana and Bhima and Manthara and Hanuman out of the way.'

Nachiket: 'What's left to be said about them?'

Lopamudra: 'Plenty! Envy. Resentment. Strength. Respect. Actually, just a little more on Bhima. I'm going to tell you a story about strength and satisfaction.'

Nachiket: 'Okay. Gargi should be here by then. I'm hungry.'

Lopamudra: 'This story is about appetites too ...'

The House of Kuru is clearly divided between the sons of Dhritarashtra and the sons of Pandu. The eldest sons from both branches of the family—Duryodhana and Yudhishtra—believe they have a claim to the throne. The ninety-nine brothers of Duryodhana and Yudhishtra's four align their loyalties. The harried mothers—Gandhari and Kunti—fail in their attempts to foster fraternal bonds. Dhritarashtra then finds a seemingly amicable solution. He decides to build a separate palace for his brother's family. The hedges in between will keep the relationships green, he hopes.

Dhritarashtra gets a palace built for the Pandavas in Varanavata. The Kauravas' motives are suspect, though. The palace is built of wax so that it can be burnt to cinders as soon as the occupants move in. However, Vidur helps the Pandavas escape from the burning palace into the forest, along with Kunti.

They finally take refuge in the house of a kind family in Ekachakra village. This village is tormented by a demon called Bakasura; actually, by the insatiable appetite of Bakasura. The villagers have made a pact with him that they will send a victim once a fortnight to his cave, to be eaten along with a cartload of assorted food. That way, the rest of them can live in a pall of 'peace'. Each household takes turns to willingly sacrifice a member. On the day that the Pandavas' hosts are to send someone on this suicidal mission, Kunti declares that it will be her son Bhima who goes instead.

Bhima reaches the mouth of the cave and begins to eat the food himself. Bakasura is enraged. He attacks him. Bhima staves him off till he has finished the cartload of food. Then, the demon and the Pandava engage in a brutal fight. Needless to say, Bakasura meets his end.

Nachiket: 'Hmmm ... So Bhima kills Bakasura. Strength—of character, I presume—vanquishes uncontrolled appetite.'

Lopamudra: 'You too! Usually it's Baba and your wife who love to grab my punchlines. But yes. It's interesting that Bhima was given the task. He was the Pandava famous for his own voracious appetite. But then, there's only one way to kill the appetite of the animal Bakasura in us—with our capacity to be more than the sum of our desires. As Bhima showed.'

Dharma Raj: 'Potential capacity, you mean. It remains untapped in many. Not in my daughter, of course. Not you either, Ketu! Others!'

Lopamudra laughed. So did Nachiket.

Nachiket: 'Aai, right now, my unsatisfied appetite is killing me. Can we eat? She'll join us soon enough.'

Dharma Raj: 'There are other types of appetite too, as you know. And our epics speak of these. Like sex.'

Lopamudra threw a surprised look at her husband. Nachiket's eyes flew to his mother-in-law's face, embarrassed.

'Namaskar, Baba. *Aai, kashi aahes tu?* How are you? Hey, Kit!' Gargi called out from near the marigold patch at the gate. 'I've got some missal pau.' She pulled down her mask as she walked up the steps and made her way indoors, past her parents and husband.

Nachiket and Lopamudra got up and followed Gargi inside. Dharma Raj remained seated on his swing, looking into the distance.

Nachiket set out the placemats while Gargi and Lopamudra heated the khichdi and missal pau in the kitchen. He was placing the containers of dahi, ghee and pickle on the table when he heard Gargi coming towards the dining room.

'Aai, would Baba mind if I had some wine with my dinner? It's been a long day. I left a bottle of Sula in your cupboard a couple of months back. It would go well with the missal pau.'

Lopamudra: 'Why not, Garu?'

Gargi placed the missal pau on the table and moved toward her parents' bedroom. Lopamudra continued, 'I don't see why Baba should mind. He is in the mood to be expansive today, I can tell. A while back, he even started on the subject of sex with Nachiket.'

'WHAT?' Gargi exclaimed, stopping in her tracks and whirling around, forgetting all about the wine. 'You guys were discussing sex? Kit, what exactly have you been talking about with my parents?'

Nachiket: 'Mahabharata. Meluha. Ramayana.'

Gargi shrugged. 'Okay. Whatever.'

Nachiket: 'I'll go fetch Baba.'

'I'm here already,' remarked Dharma Raj, as he walked in and sat down on a chair.

Gargi: 'You were talking about the Gods earlier, Baba?'

Lopamudra walked towards them with the khichdi. 'Not at all! We were talking about life. And ourselves. Discovering ourselves.'

Gargi: 'I'm sure Kit prefers to remain undiscovered!'

Dharma Raj: 'We would all prefer that, perhaps. Discover ourselves in private, if at all. But it needn't be lonely, this process of uncovering the self. It could even be propelled by characters from stories, the great epics. They introduce us to our inner drama.'

Gargi: 'So you were discussing Shiva, and the Mahabharata and the Ramayana? Which version? The Mahabharata of Veda Vyasa or B.R. Chopra? The Bengali version or the Kashmiri? There are some Sanskrit plays by Bhasa which are quite different from the mainstream versions. And which of the Ramayanas anyway—Valmiki or Tulsidas? Or Kamba Ramayanam? Or the Cambodian Reamker? Shiva of the Skanda Purana or the Shiva Purana? Or Kalidasa's Kumarasambhava? A bewildering number of versions exist, often at odds with each other and riddled with contradictions ...'

Nachiket laughed. 'There she goes. The rule maker. The marker of limits ...'

Lopamudra shrugged. 'She has a point.'

Dharma Raj: 'The number of versions isn't really the

point. The stories, and the learnings they offer, are the point. That's what makes these stories great. They are not "riddled" with contradictions; the contradictions are the point. But, if you insist, we can pick two of the most widely watched and read series in recent times, the screen version by B.R. Chopra and the novels of Amish.'

Gargi: 'Yes. I am familiar with those two. The rest are just titles for me, unfortunately.'

Dharma Raj: 'Gargi, you must understand that we are not discussing those particular stories or people. Don't lose yourself in them. They are just a means to an end. Your mother said earlier that when we cut through the surface, we touch wisdom.'

Lopamudra: 'Yes, don't think of the characters in the stories as people. They are ideas. And they are us. Our virtues. Our vices. Our strengths and weaknesses. Shift the lens.'

Nachiket: 'Aai, really, that was an important shift you helped me make. Enjoy the stories, but don't stop there. Don't get lost in them. Go deeper. Touch the wisdom and understand yourself. It doesn't matter whether the stories are from the traditional texts or their modern retellings.'

Gargi laughed. 'Hmmm. So talking about Meluha or Mahabharata is not the same as talking about Meluha or Mahabharata. Kit, you remember watching *Lakshya* with Navin and Anu?'

Lopamudra: 'The movie?'

Gargi: 'Yes, the Hrithik Roshan–Preity Zinta one. It annoyed Navin, particularly the way they depicted the Kargil War. I said to him … Kit, do you remember what I said to him?'

Nachiket: 'Do I have the guts to forget anything you've ever said?'

Gargi scrunched her nose at him and continued, 'I said to him, "The movie was not about the Kargil War at all!"'

Nachiket: 'That was funny, actually. Navin gaped at her in amazement and said, in his usual, polite fashion, "Then what was it about, pray tell?"'

Dharma Raj: 'What did you say?'

Gargi: 'I told him it was a moving tale of a wastrel, a drifter, who torturously finds his purpose in life—against the backdrop of the Kargil War.'

Lopamudra: 'You're so right. It was an emotional, coming-of-age movie. Very deeply personal.'

Dharma Raj: 'Garu, we were discussing the connected ideas of karma and dharma. Trying to shed light on them, considering how difficult they are to comprehend.'

Gargi: 'All right. So, whose lives are you going to dissect in order to comprehend them better? And which stories—Mahabharata or Ramayana or Meluha?'

Lopamudra: 'It's *what*, not *who*, we'll talk about. Baba was thinking about sex as a point of entry. That could be interesting. Sex and love.'

Gargi Sawant raised her eyebrows and smiled uncertainly. Her parents never stopped surprising her. She served herself some more missal. 'That sounds interesting, Baba. But after dinner, please.'

Nachiket shook his head at her imperceptibly.

4

LISTEN TO
YOUR HEART

It was a day for intimacy. A day when the family dropped some inhibitions. The older couple and their daughter poured themselves a glass of wine each. Nachiket held back, but not entirely. He sank into the leather armchair and said, 'Baba, you started an interesting conversation back there, about other appetites.'

Gargi sprang to her feet. 'Kit, let me get you some hot chocolate.'

'Sit, sit. In a moment,' her husband said.

Dharma Raj: 'Well, at one end of the spectrum of sexuality, there is Bhishma, with his celibacy. At the other end is Dushasana, with his lustful excesses.'

Lopamudra: 'And who would be in the middle then, somewhere between these two extremes?'

Dharma Raj: 'Bhima and Arjuna. Remember, one kills Dushasana. The other kills Bhishma.'

Lopamudra: 'If we're talking about sensuality and love, not just sex, I can also think of Parvateshwar and Anandmayi. But you go first.'

Dharma Raj: 'Garu, we had discussed Bhishma

earlier, as the embodiment of pointless sacrifice. A selfish, self-filled sacrifice, isn't that what you called it, Lopa? Well, Bhishma also embodies the idea of celibacy. Such big words: sacrifice, celibacy. Some would say they deserve no further examination. But, to my mind, they're like two exalted beings sitting on the pedestal of moral arrogance. You know that Bhishma denied himself sensuality. But it was a selfish embrace of selflessness. His so-called sacrifice caused the conflict in the family.'

Lopamudra: 'You're right. He was irresponsible. The thing is, there are no clear lines that separate right from wrong in this story. Like we discussed earlier, if you renounce your desires self-righteously, it may be because you have a desire to be seen to be "great". Often, high-minded people sit on the sidelines and pontificate while "lesser" men tackle the problems on the ground.'

Gargi: 'And what does that have to do with celibacy?'

Dharma Raj: 'Sexual denial can breed celibate arrogance. You start feeling superior.'

Lopamudra: 'Maybe that arrogance existed in Parvateshwar as well. Certainly, the first time he encountered Anandmayi.'

'I don't think so. The first time, he was plain gobsmacked!' Gargi laughed.

The Chandravanshi Swadweepans and Suryavanshi Meluhans fight a great battle. The Meluhans are led by Shiva and Parvateshwar, and the Swadweepans by Prince Bhagirath. The mighty Chandravanshis are reduced to stragglers fighting for a lost cause. But Shiva is troubled in the wake of this comprehensive victory. He had met Emperor Dilipa of Swadweep and watched the proud man crumble in agony when he realised who Shiva was. Shiva is wracked by guilt. He has not destroyed evil. The Chandravanshis are different, not evil.

Into this setting is injected the ravishing Anandmayi, princess of Swadweep. She is an unabashed epicurean and an embodiment of beauty, sensuality, boldness and passion. She does not mince her words. She displays her temper when angered. And she does not hide her attraction for the dour Meluhan general, Parvateshwar. He is appalled, but also destabilised. He blushes profusely as Anandmayi scans him like she would an exquisite piece of art. She flirts with him outrageously while he hides his confusion and dread behind a brusque, surly demeanour.

Anandmayi wants this man. And thus begins her dogged pursuit of the reluctant Parvateshwar. Until he surrenders.

Gargi: 'Later, when she entered Shiva's tent and threw a casual "How are you doing, Parvateshwar" at him, he actually blushed! Can you imagine Bhishma embarrassed or blushing furiously?'

Lopamudra: 'Hmmm, that's true. Intentions make all the difference. Bona fides—Baba's favourite word. The hidden intention or motive behind Bhishma's celibacy is moral arrogance and grandstanding. Shantanu was an old man. Satyavati's father's demands were unreasonable and selfish. On the other hand, Parvateshwar's vow of celibacy was based on a deep sense of honour. Doubly so, because he was abiding by his grandfather's decision.'

Gargi: 'Ma, you mentioned a hidden intention. What does that mean? Did Bhishma hide his real intention from his father? His family?'

Lopamudra: 'His real intentions were hidden from himself. Our conscious mind is very clever. It creates honourable motives for our private consumption, which we earnestly believe. But beneath the pretence of awareness lie our real intentions. They remain dormant for all but the most courageous among us—those who have the courage to face their face!'

Dharma Raj: 'Questioning ourselves and establishing bona fides for our thoughts and actions is a deep exercise. We must talk about it someday.'

Gargi: 'Not today. I'm getting sucked into the lives of these people! So, Bhishma honoured his father's base instincts, and Parvateshwar honoured his grandfather's honourable act. Both were celibate men. The act was the same, the essence could not have been more different. And yet, who or what could vanquish this idea of abstinence being applause-worthy?'

'Arjuna, of course. Right, Raj?' Lopamudra looked at her husband. 'We'll come to Anandmayi later. There's no vice to be killed in her case. Only a virtue to be drawn out.'

Dharma Raj gestured for her to continue.

Lopamudra: 'Arjuna accepted his sensuality. And the resultant joy. He was at ease with it. He found love in many exemplary women: Ulupi, Chitrangada, Subhadra. His women were learned and capable, and they gave birth to accomplished sons: Iravan, Babruvahana, Abhimanyu ...'

Ulupi is the widowed daughter of a Naga called Kauravya of the Airavata clan. Smitten with Arjuna, she proposes marriage to him. They have a son called Iravan, who will one day play an important role on the battleground of Kurukshetra. And still later, in modern India, he will be honoured as the patron God of transpersons, especially in Tamil Nadu.

Chitrangada is the warrior princess of Manipur. Also smitten with Arjuna, she courts him. They are allowed to marry, provided that any children they have will remain with King Manivahana, her father. Prince Babhruvahana remains in Manipur as heir to the throne. He too will play a crucial role in the Great War.

Krishna's sister, Subhadra, knows that her elder brother Balarama wants her to marry Duryodhana. But she is in love with Arjuna. During his travels, Arjuna finally arrives in Krishna's city, Dwaraka. And Subhadra elopes with the man she loves.

Draupadi is the common wife of the Pandavas. On Krishna's advice, she spends one year exclusively with each brother. The men are free to marry others and find companionship during the four years she is not with them. But she lays down a condition: that the other wives will not live in Indraprastha. However, Subhadra manages to charm her, and Draupadi allows her to live in the city. Arjuna and Subhadra give birth to a mighty son, Abhimanyu.

Abhimanyu's story is gut-wrenching. On the thirteenth day of the Great Battle, Drona devises a menacing plan. With Arjuna away at the other end of the battlefield, he organises his soldiers in a

Chakravyuh, a battle formation that slowly squeezes the enemy into the centre of an intricate trap. The Pandavas are encircled. And so is Abhimanyu.

Many years ago, when Subhadra was pregnant, she had asked Arjuna to describe this battle formation to her. Alas, as Arjuna's explanation reached a crucial stage, Subhadra fell asleep. The young lad in her womb only learned how to breach the formation and help others escape. Not how to get out himself, at the end. And so he helps his family breach the formation, and they promise to return with reinforcements and rescue him.

But Jayadhrata, Duryodhana's brother-in-law, blocks the efforts of the Pandavas. Young Abhimanyu is trapped alone. He fights like a lion, but is killed by his uncles and cousins.

Gargi: 'Abhimanyu was particularly grand. What a lion of a man!'

Nachiket: 'But we're talking about Mufasa, not Simba.'

Lopamudra: 'What's that?'

Gargi: 'It's a movie, Aai. *The Lion King*. Do see it. You two would enjoy it. Abhimanyu is the Simba to Arjuna's Mufasa. *Chakravyuh* means a *labyrinth*, doesn't it?'

Nachiket: 'Yes. It's rich in symbolism. Like the labyrinth of Theseus, built by Daedalus.'

Lopamudra: 'Well, getting back to your Mufasa and my Arjuna ... His sensuality was controlled. It didn't lapse into lust at any point.'

Gargi: 'On what basis do you say that?'

Lopamudra: 'During his travels, Arjuna visited his father, Lord Indra, king of the Devas and ruler of the skies. Arjuna spent his days and nights immersed in the pleasures that heaven offered him. He enjoyed the company of the heavenly *Apsaras*, the *celestial nymphs*. One day, the beautiful Urvashi expressed a desire to be his lover. But Arjuna turned her down. He had his reasons.'

Dharma Raj: 'When sensuality is mindful, it is distinct from lust. Because lust is mindless. When Arjuna turned her down, Urvashi threatened to lay a curse on him. He remained steadfast. She, on the other hand, was willing to forget that he was her descendant.'

Nachiket: 'One is mindful, the other is mindless. That's the key difference.'

Gargi: 'So Arjuna goes around sowing his seed; mindfully, I grant. He is picky-choosy. Are you also saying then that it's okay for a man to love more than one woman?'

Lopamudra: 'This is the Mahabharata, Garu. Draupadi lived with five men. And she loved them all, didn't she? Is that okay? Not okay? Good stories offer no prescriptions. We must figure these things out on our own. And, whatever the choice we make, we must live with the consequences. That's all.'

Dharma Raj: 'You are being mindful when you pull back from crossing certain lines. It does not matter what those lines are; that's a matter of detail. The ancient masters of spirituality were more interested in the internal life, in the mind. In emotions, sensations, thoughts, energy. These are the tools that control our choices and experiences. Once we decode these tools, we can take control of our actions, at least in the external sense. The ancient texts speak of a time when wise people did not judge. They observed the world and those around them. They observed themselves. They converted these observations into lessons and used them to improve their inner life.'

Nachiket: 'They were the world's first philosophers.'

Dharma Raj: 'True. But let us get back to Arjuna and Bhishma. Lopa?'

Lopamudra: 'Okay. So, one way to look at this is that the tool that Arjunic sensuality uses to "kill" celibate arrogance is a philosophical shunning of denial. Arjuna used Shikhandi to kill Bhishma.'

The king of Kashi organises a swayamvar for his three daughters, Amba, Ambika and Ambalika. Vichitravirya, the weak son of Shantanu and Satyavati, is not sent an invitation. Bhishma, his stepbrother, takes offense on behalf of the House of Kuru. He rides to Kashi and kidnaps the three princesses. On reaching home, they are presented to Vichitravirya as his brides.

But Amba, the eldest, is unwilling. She had intended to pick her lover, Shalva, during the swayamvar. Bhishma allows her to leave. Shalva, however, will not have her after she has been kidnapped and offered to another man. The hapless Amba returns to Hastinapura and demands that Bhishma marry her as recompense for wrecking her life. But Bhishma, of course, has taken the oath of celibacy.

Amba kills herself, but not before swearing to become the cause of Bhishma's death in her next life. She is reborn as Shikhandi, child of Drupada and sibling to Draupadi. Shikhandi is born female but later changes into a man. As foretold, on the tenth day of the Great War, she/he becomes the cause of Bhishma's death.

Dharma Raj: 'Amba/Shikhandi is the embodiment of love that is denied. Do not spurn love insensitively. Do not ride roughshod over matters of the heart. Such love can become toxic. And toxicity kills. Sometimes, literally!'

Gargi: 'Parvateshwar did not spurn love, na? He didn't insult or abuse anyone.'

There is more to Anandmayi than her stunning beauty. She is devastated when she realises that Shiva the Neelkanth, the prophesied saviour, has sided with the Meluhans. He is meant to be on the Swadweepan's side, the 'good' side! Her resilience makes her bounce back. She tells Shiva that he has been misled by the evil Suryavanshis.

Parvateshwar is perturbed. She throws her first philosophical salvo at him and rocks his linear mind. 'Why couldn't Lord Ram have been both Suryavanshi and Chandravanshi?' she asks. The general is confused.

Later, a riot breaks out in the Branga quarter in Kashi. The hapless Brangas are surrounded by a hostile Kashi mob. Parvateshwar devises a courageous plan to save the Brangas, but is grievously injured in the ensuing melee. It is a head injury. Anandmayi refuses to leave his bedside. And Parvateshwar is torn by desire.

Much later, the citizens of Kashi organise a celebration to honour the birth of Kartik, the son of Shiva. Anandmayi choreographs a beautiful duet: the dance of Vishwamitra and Menaka. She performs it with Uttanka, who is restricted by a hump on his right shoulder—the result of a battle injury. It restricts his arm movements and requires that the two dancers move closely, in unison. Anandmayi wants to make her general jealous. She succeeds.

When she realises that he deeply appreciates military valour and skill, she learns to wield a knife, and Parvateshwar watches her target practise like a trained warrior. The knives hit the target dead centre. She also learns to wield the long sword. Parvateshwar is filled with admiration.

He tells her that he is sworn to celibacy. It's a family pact. She is finally helpless. She knows now how he feels.

Parvateshwar then turns to Shiva, but hesitates to ask. Shiva reaches out and clears his mind. It is simple. Shiva tells him, 'Listen to your heart. In the name of Lord Ram, go to her!'

Gargi: 'I love the way he melts, slowly but surely. As for Anandmayi, I totally adore her! She knew how to pursue him. When direct enticement didn't work, she took to dance. When that too failed, she took to warriorship. When he was lying prone, unconscious, injured during the riots in the Branga quarters, she touched him with love. Yet, he struggled. When she danced with Uttanka, too close for comfort, he felt the fire of jealousy. When she impressed him with her knife-wielding skills on the way to the gates of Branga, he offered to duel with her as a sign of fellowship. Sweet!'

Lopamudra: 'He struggled with his vows. He was human, more connected to his emotions, unlike Bhishma.'

Gargi: 'When he explained to her why he was celibate, she said something poignant: that a good man had rebelled against injustice in a faraway land, two hundred and fifty years ago. Today, that rebellion had brought injustice to her! He smiled softly as he listened to her. Later, when Shiva told him to listen to his heart, he did. He broke his vow because, as Shiva told him, it would serve the purpose of justice.'

Dharma Raj: 'Maybe Bhishma never met a woman he could admire and respect. And adore.'

Gargi: 'Amba was worthy enough! Granted, she didn't love Bhishma. But, if he hadn't been blind to

other truths beyond his own vow of celibacy, he may
have been able to give her justice. On that spectrum of
sexuality we spoke of earlier, celibacy weighed down by
moral arrogance is certainly one undesirable extreme.
And Bhishma epitomises that.'

Gargi: 'You located Dushasana at the other extreme,
didn't you? His lustful disrobing of Draupadi in the
royal court.'

Dharma Raj: 'Have you heard of Sarala Das?'

Nachiket: 'A character in the Mahabharata?'

Lopamudra: 'Ketuuuuu ... *kaaye bolat aahes?* What
are you saying? He's a fifteenth-century Odia poet. So,
what about him, Raj?'

Dharma Raj: 'Sarala Das has written a scholarly
exposition of the Mahabharata. And he suggests that
poor Dushasana was "helpless" as he was only obeying
his elder brother.'

Gargi: 'Duryodhana ...'

Nachiket: 'Many molesters and rapists say they were
helpless.'

Gargi: 'Yeah. "The devil got into me. I couldn't
control myself. It wasn't my fault." Hazaar excuses are
spouted.'

Dharma Raj: 'And all such excuses are inexcusable.'

Dushasana is the second son of Gandhari and Dhritarashtra. From childhood, he shadows his older brother, Duryodhana. He loves him, admires him, and obeys him unquestioningly. His dedication does not falter even when Karna becomes his brother's most trusted friend.

The Kauravas invite the Pandavas to Hastinapura for a game of dice. Gambling is Yudhishtra's great vice. The game is played by Yudhishtra and Shakuni on behalf of the Pandavas and the Kauravas respectively. Shakuni, Gandhari's brother, has schemed to arrange the match. On the throw of the dice, Yudhishtra loses his possessions, including all his wealth and land. A compulsive gambler, he cannot stop. He stakes and loses his brothers, one by one. He stakes himself and loses. He shamelessly stakes Draupadi, their wife. And loses.

Duryodhana asks Dushasana to fetch their sister-in-law, forcefully if need be. Duryodhana has a bone to pick with her. She had once called him the blind son of a blind man. Dushasana drags Draupadi into the gambling hall. Duryodhana commands his younger brother to disrobe the haughty wife of the Pandavas. Dushasana does not demur. He begins to pull her sari from one end.

Draupadi cries out to Krishna for help. How can he not respond? Magically, her sari continues to unravel, without an end. Dushasana keeps pulling, but Draupadi remains covered. Dushasana does not stop. He has his excuse. He is helpless, after all. He is only obeying his brother.

Nachiket: 'The ever-obedient Dushasana. I never thought of him that way. Obedience can be such a convenient excuse. It's convenient to feel helpless. You can throw up your hands and not accept any responsibility ... But what conquers lust, then?'

Gargi: 'Let me first tell you what will never conquer lust. Celibacy! Sex is a biological need. If you deny it, it will torment you, non-stop, at the back of your mind, as much as physically.'

Nachiket: 'Anirban ...'

Gargi: 'Yes, tell us what Anirban would say! Mr Know-it-all!'

Lopamudra: 'He sounds like a nice guy, Garu. Don't you like him?'

Gargi: 'He's nice, Aai. I just wish my husband enjoyed my company half as much!'

Nachiket: 'That's popcorn outrage, Baba. Stop looking so distressed!'

Gargi laughed. 'So where's my popcorn, wise guy? Anyway, tell us what he said. He always says interesting things, I grant you.'

Nachiket: 'You enjoy his company even more than I do! For some reason I can't remember now, Anirban was talking to me about the early Christians. St Augustine recorded his private struggles with his sexuality with great honesty in his memoir. Astonishing, for those times. Then there was St Paul, *ter* Jesus *cha* apostle *hota*; he was one of the apostles, the thirteenth apostle, actually. He wrote about his agony in his letters ...'

St Augustine is born to a Christian woman and a pagan father in the fourth century AD. It is a time of flux, when the old ways of life are giving way to Christianity, which is gradually gaining acceptance. He is educated in the classical philosophies of Homer and Plato, and converts to Christianity in Rome, when he is thirty-two. His most famous work is *Confessions*, in which he is astonishingly honest about himself. He forcefully condemns his bodily desires that refuse to release him from their grip. He most certainly does not know inner peace for large parts of his life.

St Paul's life has a different trajectory. As is well known, there were twelve disciples in Jesus' lifetime.

St Paul is born a Jew in Tarsus, modern-day Turkey. He is one of the earliest persecutors of Christians but also among the first generation of Christians. He converts to Christianity after an incident on a road to Damascus. He sees a bright light and falls to the ground. A voice calls out to him, and Jesus appears in a vision. 'The road to Damascus' has since become a phrase that signifies a watershed moment in a person's life.

St Paul spends the rest of his life travelling the world and spreading the message of Jesus. But his internal life is tumultuous. So mortified is he by the needs of his body that he wishes he could be rid of it. He writes extensively on the need to control the sexual impulse.

Dharma Raj: 'I wonder whether Anirban the internationalist knows that Mahatma Gandhi also acknowledged a similar anguish. Sexual energy is compulsive and difficult to ignore or control. In fact, most organised religions see it as a roadblock to spiritual growth.'

Lopamudra: 'But there are also those who see it differently. Sex is not only an expression of love, it's also a gateway to the divine. It's sacred.'

Gargi: 'It's at the root of creation, after all.'

Nachiket: 'At the risk of repetition, what "kills" lust?'

Lopamudra: 'Love, of course. It works like a glue in any relationship. Bhima's love for Draupadi was special. He was the one who truly loved her. And Draupadi knew this. When she needed protection, she turned to him.'

Gargi: 'Like when Kichaka stalked her.'

The Pandavas are exiled for twelve years after the game of dice. They must live in hiding in the thirteenth year, after which they can return home. In that thirteenth year, they arrive in disguise to work in the palace of King Virata of Matsya. Yudhishtra becomes Kanka, advisor to the king; Bhima is Ballava, the cook; Arjuna is Brihanalla, an accomplished female dancer; Nakula is Damagranth, a horse groomer; Sahadeva is Tantipala, a physician; and Draupadi becomes Sairandhri, the queen's maid.

The queen's brother, Kichaka, takes a shine to Sairandhri, and stalks her with increasing boldness. Sudeshna, the queen, is immune to her pleas. Sairandhri goes to the kitchens and speaks to Ballava. Ballava, or Bhima, kills Kichaka brutally. It blows their cover, but Bhima is the husband who comes to the aid of his wife.

Lopamudra: 'Earlier, when Dushasana humiliated her in front of the elders, she leaned on Bhima to quench her thirst for revenge. She knew that her pain was his pain. That he would not rest till he had avenged her.'

Dharma Raj: 'Bhima drank Dushasana's blood. The mode of killing is important.'

Lopamudra: 'Totally, Raj. Love overwhelms and destroys lust. Lust can be overpowering. It can be very difficult for love to rein it in and bring it under control. Sometimes, the sincerest efforts fail in a blind moment of lapse. Whereas fidelity can be immensely rewarding over time.'

Dharma Raj: 'True. Life is essentially about rising above our animal nature. We must realise the potential of being human, in one lifetime or the other. That's when we can experience the true beauty of companionship.'

Lopamudra: 'The Tantra Shastra is misunderstood these days, but it is an exploration along these lines. Anyway, spiritual union is rarely experienced through the denial of sex. Enjoy it and be done with it. Don't deny it. Don't get trapped in it either.'

Dharma Raj: 'Look at the horrific cases of paedophilia among Catholic priests around the world that we've been reading about. It's shaking the foundations of the Vatican. Even if you manage to control your actions, the thought of sex can get stuck in your head. Like with St Paul.'

Gargi: 'Osho says that love first expresses itself through the body, as sex. Then through the mind, as love. And then through the spirit, as prayer.'

Dharma Raj: 'Eventually, it leads to the soul uniting with the Absolute, like when Meerabai disappears into the image of Lord Krishna.'

Nachiket: 'On that wonderful note, would anyone care for my special hot chocolate?'

Gargi: 'Oh no, I was supposed to get it for you! I forgot. Let me help you make it.'

The younger couple rose and went indoors.

5

THE CASE
FOR HUMILITY

'I'm so sorry I forgot your hot chocolate,' Gargi said, reaching over to hug Nachiket.

Nachiket smiled and manoeuvred himself out of reach. 'It's all right. Forget about it. Forgetting is easy, na? And always understandable.' Behind the smile was a subtle sulk she was familiar with.

Gargi turned away and opened the glass cabinet in which the cups were kept. Nachiket lit the burner and placed a pan on it, then opened the fridge and took out a container of milk. Gargi placed the tin of hot chocolate next to the burner. As Nachiket poured the milk into the pan, Gargi placed a spoon next to the chocolate. Nachiket's face softened. Gargi opened the fridge and found the Tetra Pak containing cream. Nachiket usually avoided adding cream in his hot chocolate, but Dharma Raj loved that final, sinful dash. Nachiket smiled and reached for his wife. She melted into him and wound her arms around his waist. They stood, rocking gently, watching the milk come to a boil. It was the end of a practised dance of love: she forgot; he chose to forget that she forgot.

Fifteen minutes later, Gargi and Nachiket entered the living room with two mugs each. Gargi handed one to her father. 'Here's my husband's famous hot chocolate. He's mighty proud of it.'

Nachiket jumped in before his father-in-law could reply. 'What about pride, Baba? I think of Parvateshwar when I think of pride. Honourable pride.'

Dharma Raj took a sip and smiled. 'Very nice, Ketu. Okay, so there are types and types of pride. There's pride as a badge of honour, yes. Think of Parvateshwar. There's magnificent pride. Think of Lady Sati. And then there is injured pride. Drona. Injured pride can be corrosive, but there is an antidote to it: humility. It counters the prickliness of an injured ego. Guru Dronacharya represents injured pride and Yudhishtra represents humility.'

Lopamudra: 'Yes, I see what you mean about Drona. He's the epitome of injured pride. But Yudhishtra? Everyone thinks he's humble, but is that what humility is? Being passive and ineffective? How is that a desirable quality?'

Nachiket: 'I agree with Aai. I think Yudhishtra was just weak. That's it.'

Gargi: 'Actually, I don't get how Drona represents pride either.'

Lopamudra: 'Let me take this one, Raj. You can tell

us about Yudhishtra afterwards. I'd love to hear you unpeel his humility.'

Dharma Raj: 'All right.'

Lopamudra: 'So, Drona. As you know, he was a warrior and a priest. He tutored the Kaurava and Pandava princes in the art of war.'

Drona, the son of Rishi Bharadwaja, is married to Kripi. They have a son called Ashwatthama. Being extremely poor, they cannot afford to keep a cow. And it pains Kripi that her son does not know the taste of milk. She knows that Drupada, king of Panchala, is a childhood friend of her husband. She pleads with Drona to ask him for help.

Drona visits him and recalls an old promise that Drupada had made to him when they were children: that the king would share his wealth with his poor friend. Drona does not desire the king's wealth. All he asks for is a cow to feed his deprived child.

Drupada scoffs at his former friend and says that they were both immature children at the time, that real friendship can only be among equals. Drupada is a king now and Drona a minor priest. The king will certainly give him a cow, but as charity. Drona has no grounds to stake a claim on anything from him while retaining his dignity at the same time. He stands before the king a beggar.

Dharma Raj: 'Drupada scorned Drona when he reached out to him for help. A person's self-esteem can shatter when he is publicly mocked. It was not such a big deal, you know. He was just asking for a cow. And Drupada, his friend, was a wealthy king.'

Lopamudra: 'He didn't reach out for help. He demanded help. Drupada may have made him a promise, but to demand help like that, so many years later, was graceless. And yes, insults hurt. But wounded pride can be poisonous. For the "aggressee", not the aggressor.'

Nachiket: 'I hate to admit it, but you have a point. I feel for the guy, though.'

Gargi: 'I agree with you, Ma. If you must ask for something, ask gracefully. Without qualifications. Grant that the person you are asking has the right to be honest in his response. And why should asking for help be against one's dignity? Injured pride is built on a swollen ego. Remember the grace with which the beggar offered his food to Shiva, on the way to the Ram Janmabhoomi temple in Ayodhya?'

The *dharmayudh* has been won by the great army of Shiva and Parvateshwar. The evil Chandravanshis have been vanquished by the righteous Suryavanshis. But then, Shiva has a stunning epiphany among the people of Swadweep—the Island of the Individual. He discovers that this was not a *dharmayudh* after all. That Meluha—the Land of Pure Life—has picked up cudgels against a people who are freedom-loving and self-willed, not evil.

Shiva is beset by guilt and remorse. The death of thousands of soldiers weighs heavily on his conscience, as do the accusing, pain-filled eyes of Emperor Dilipa and Princess Anandmayi. Grief-stricken, he walks up the hill towards the Ram Janmabhoomi temple. Lord Ram will guide him. Soothe him. Help him find some answers. He begins to softly repeat the name of the Lord. Ram. Ram. Ram. Ram.

Farther up, he comes upon an old, shrivelled man on the roadside, who seems to have not eaten in weeks and is dressed in tatters. On his leg, an ankle wound festers from neglect and the humidity. He holds a banana leaf precariously in his left hand. On it is some bread and gruel. Shiva is consumed by sudden anger. This beggar suffers almost at the foot of Lord Ram's temple. The kingdom should be looking after him. Meluha would have! It has enough food for all. The old man would not have had to endure such humiliation in the Land of the Pure. He knows now that Parvateshwar is right. The Chandravanshis lead a wretched existence. Maybe he has not made such a terrible mistake after all.

But fate conspires to deny Shiva this small consolation. The old man meets Shiva's gaze with compassion and openness. He is at peace with himself. He mistakes Shiva's keen look for hunger and invites him to share his meal. 'Would you like to eat with me, my son? There is enough for both of us. Sit with me,' he says. When Shiva hesitates, the old man shrinks back, his pride hurt. 'This is good food,' he says. Shiva has wounded him by treating him like a beggar!

Shiva sits beside the man on the pavement. The old man places the banana leaf on the ground, beaming with joy. Shiva places the first morsel in his mouth. It slips into his body easily, but weighs heavily upon his soul. His righteousness is squeezed out of him by the man's astounding generosity. The food is over in no time.

Freedom. Freedom that also offers dignity. For all. This would have been impossible in Meluha.

The old man smiles affectionately and bids him goodbye. 'Go. It's a long walk to the temple.'

How could Shiva have thought that he could 'save' this wonderful man?

Gargi: 'Shiva accepted the offering with grace and humility. The old man did beg for a living, but he had the magnificent pride of a man who was at peace with himself and his circumstances. If the giver exhibits generosity, the taker can also show generosity of spirit.'

Nachiket: 'But Drupada scorned Drona.'

Gargi: 'I wonder what the real trigger was: the scornful denial or the initial ask? Drupada may have reacted very differently had he not been asked with such a sense of entitlement. On his own, he may have remembered his promise and reduced his friend's discomfiture. Grace evokes grace. It builds a virtuous cycle.'

Lopamudra: 'Humility is the antidote, of course. Which brings us to Yudhishtra. Tell us, Raj.'

Dharma Raj: 'Well, Yudhishtra arranged Drona's death. And so, if you extend the metaphor, humility killed injured pride. In theory, we are all capable of humility. But humble people can also be very self-righteous, especially if they are weak. In that case, their humility does not translate into practice. In fact, it can be quite the opposite in practice.'

Nachiket: 'Hmmm ... so humility is an escape for the weak and a choice for the strong?'

Gargi: 'It isn't humility at all then. Tactical humility is cunning.'

Dharma Raj: 'And often useful. Circumstances can place even the strongest people in a position of weakness. Do not be judgemental, ever.'

Lopamudra: 'Especially with those who exhibit weakness. There are worse things to be than weak.'

Dharma Raj: 'Getting back to Yudhishtra ... I think of him as a classic Part One and Part Two character.'

Yudhishtra is the son of Yama, the God of death and dharma. He sincerely follows the path of dharma. He never fails to speak up for what he thinks is right—words are easy. When Karna wants to exhibit his skills in a tournament organised by Drona, Yudhishtra immediately objects. In his understanding of dharma at the time, a charioteer's son has no claim to Kshatriya merit, however worthy he may be. Yudhishtra will not admit it, even to himself, but he stands in Arjuna's corner. Dharma can be convenient too.

He slips up when situations demand more than words. For he is a man with weaknesses. Gambling, for instance. He accepts the Kauravas' invitation to a game of dice. Shakuni is the master of the game; everyone knows that. But Shakuni is even more masterful when it comes to understanding human nature. He knows Yudhishtra cannot resist. One by one, the stakes of the game rise. Blinded by his addiction, Yudhishtra stakes all. And loses all.

Such is his weakness that, even after Draupadi's humiliation, when asked to play a final game, he returns to the board. He is sure he will win this time. The classic gambler's fallacy. But, of course, he loses. And they are exiled for thirteen years.

Transformation requires guidance, introspection and self-examination. Yudhishtra submits himself to these rigours during his exile in the forest. He learns that words must translate into actions. More importantly, actions must substitute words.

He learns to protect. Not with words, but with action. When a giant python squeezes Bhima in a tight coil, Yudhishtra offers himself instead. The python is, in fact, Nahusha, an ancestor, and the brothers survive unscathed.

He learns to listen. A rishi in the Kamyaka forest asks for some sticks for his ritual fire. Yudhishtra sends his brothers, one by one, but none return. So he goes in search of them. He reaches a pond and finds his brothers unconscious on the ground nearby. Feeling thirsty, he cups his hands to drink some water from the pond. And hears the voice of a Yaksha. He stops. None of the others had, and that's why they have fallen. But Yudhishtra has learned to think before he acts.

The exile ends and the Great War begins. One day, the moment of truth is upon him. Drona, the great warrior, must be brought down. They know that his son Ashwatthama's death will knock the fight out of their teacher. The problem is, Ashwatthama is alive. But if Yudhishtra says that he is dead, Drona will instantly believe him and lay down his weapons. For Yudhishtra does not lie. Or does he? What is truth? Is the opposite of truth falsehood? Is truth related to facts? To verifiable data? Or can it be the truth of intention? Not what we do, but why we do what we do. Here, the subliminal truth is that the war must end.

Yudhishtra does not hesitate. When he tells Drona that Ashwatthama has died, Drona lays down his weapons, closes his eyes and prepares for death.

Yudhishtra acts in the larger interest and faces the personal consequences.

Gargi: 'What, then, is Yudhishtra Part One?'

Dharma Raj: 'He is humble but passive. He is high-minded, but it's really just posturing, mere words. His conduct is self-indulgent and grand.'

Gargi: 'You bet! He gambled away the people he was supposed to protect!'

Dharma Raj: 'I want to take this further, Gargi. You know, the Greeks called the physical body "soma" and the inner, divine self "nous". Soma and nous are connected by "psyche", the emotional body. An unstable psyche causes a disconnect between soma and nous.'

Lopamudra: 'Which is when words don't translate into action. They become an end in themselves.'

Gargi: 'I am compassionate because I talk passionately about compassion! I am kind because I argue with my best friends on behalf of the poor. I am patriotic because I cannot stand it when a stranger does not stand up for the national anthem!'

Dharma Raj: 'Yes. There is a perceptible gap between what most of us think we are and what we really are. You say that about me, Lopa. I am not so unique, you know. It's a common affliction.'

Lopamudra: 'I'm sure it's true about me too. The way we see ourselves is very different from the way others see us. Sometimes we know what we really are, but we carefully hide it from everyone else.'

Nachiket: 'Does anyone have a completely stable psyche?'

Gargi: 'Sigmund Freud divided the psyche into the id, the ego and the super-ego. The id is the animal aspect; it's instinctive. It has desires and it demands fulfilment. Paul MacLean would locate the id in our "reptilian" and "limbic" brain.'

Nachiket: 'Who's Paul MacLean?'

Gargi: 'An American neuroscientist. He built an evolutionary model of the human brain—the triune brain. The "reptilian" brain only understands action and reaction. You cannot teach it to not react. The "limbic" brain is the place of senses and emotions. It's like a spoilt child. You cannot stop it from screaming and shouting. It must get what it wants.'

Nachiket: 'So, the id is a combination of our instinct for survival and our emotional desires. What are the ego and the super-ego?'

Gargi: 'They have nothing to do with the word "ego", which is just an inflated sense of self. Freud's super-ego is the moral authority; it's like your Greek nous, Baba.'

Dharma Raj: 'Maybe. Maybe not. The concept of nous is far more complex.'

Gargi: 'Whatever. We could call it our conscience.'

Nachiket: 'And what's the ego then, which has nothing to do with the ego?'

Gargi: 'Like Mahabharata, which has nothing to do with the Mahabharata?'

Nachiket: 'Touché!'

Lopamudra: 'Go on, Gargi.'

Gargi: 'Freud's ego is our inner Kurukshetra, the battlefield on which the id and the super-ego battle it out. The ego faces pressure from both ends. It needs to be trained and stabilised so it can reason and learn. Anyway, go on, Baba. I'm done with showing off my knowledge!'

Dharma Raj: 'I'll get back to the Greeks, if you don't mind. Freud is not my cup of tea. I would say that our thoughts and emotions need constant supervision. Or they could become unbalanced, and then soma and nous get disconnected. As in Yudhishtra's case.'

Gargi: 'Baba, would you call him a hypocrite?'

Dharma Raj: 'No, I wouldn't. Not Yudhisthra, nor any other person. Because most people are blissfully unaware of what they are really like. Their flaws are visible to others, but not to them. Yudhishtra Part One is escapist, weak, and given to addictions.'

Nachiket: 'And Part Two?'

Dharma Raj: 'Well, righteousness must be put to work; it must extend beyond words. What you profess should reflect in your conduct. If you believe in something, it should show up in your actions. The gap between our expressed values and the reality of our thoughts and actions cannot remain constant. We must keep narrowing it.'

Nachiket: 'How?'

Dharma Raj: 'Through becoming self-aware.'

Gargi: 'And you think Yudhishtra was able to do that?'

Dharma Raj: 'Yes, but it took him a long time. And a lot of hardship. Self-understanding does not come easy. It calls for an exile of sorts from our internal dramas. We all think we know ourselves, but very few actually do.'

Gargi: 'If any! Sadhguru Jaggi Vasudev says that if you ask two friends to assess you, and also two others who don't like you, you'll find that it's a cleansing process.'

Dharma Raj: 'He's right. We all want to feel good about ourselves. In theory, we agree that we are not perfect. But what does that really mean? What are our imperfections? Do we even want to know?'

Lopamudra: 'Hmmm. I agree. It's easier to delude ourselves. We even perceive others in a way that serves our own self-image. Like you said, Raj, we need to feel good about ourselves, above all else. Noticing our own flaws makes us feel bad, so we block the view. We paper over our faults. Disguise them. Re-engineer them. When we notice the flaws of others, we allow ourselves to shine in comparison. There's a strange sense of moral superiority inherent in almost everyone.'

Nachiket: 'Sometimes this creates the classic fault-finder, who doesn't know how to change anything but is filled with dissatisfaction, outrage and intolerance.'

Gargi: 'Or the classic do-gooder. And some of them do a lot of good, na?'

Lopamudra: 'Yes, but we're discussing spiritualism, not social reform or progress. Don't mix the two.'

Nachiket: 'It's true that we are all excellent advocates of our own conduct and self-righteous judges of the conduct of others.'

Lopamudra: 'We shield ourselves psychologically and focus only on our good qualities. And we all have some of those, just as others have their faults. But what about our faults and the good qualities of others? Compassion for me; judgement for those around me. It's the default approach for many.'

Gargi: 'The judgement becomes stronger when it comes to people who are not "our own". If we like someone, we don't see their flaws; if we don't like someone, we don't see any merit in them. It's the perfect feel-good recipe, and I get that. But Yudhishtra? Where does he come in?'

Dharma Raj: 'Yudhishtra understood the shortcomings of others. He was a good judge of character. But he did not have similar clarity about himself. And if at all he did, he could not exercise control over it. That's Yudhishtra Part One. Now let's move to Yudhishtra Part Two.'

Nachiket: 'Thank you, Baba. Finally!'

Dharma Raj smiled as he settled back in the armchair. 'Yudhishtra uses his humiliation to narrow the gap between what he wants to be and what he is able to be. To begin with, he attempts to truly see himself. In Part Two, we see humility and righteousness using the tool of action to slay pride.'

Lopamudra: 'Got it! Dhrishtadyumna! The tool.'

Dharma Raj looked at his wife and smiled.

Nachiket: 'Explain, you two.'

Lopamudra: 'Dhrishtadyumna was Drupada's son and Draupadi's brother. "Dhrusht" means a mighty person and "dyumna" means valour, the ability to attack. So, "Dhrishtadyumna" can be translated as the ability to take strong action. You could personify him as Daring, Courage and Action. After Yudhishtra robbed his guru of the will to live, Dhrishtadyumna beheaded him.'

Dharma Raj: 'Drona laid down his arms and prepared for death. Metaphorically, pride had lost its will to live and was participating in its own destruction.'

Nachiket: 'Here again, the manner of death is enlightening. But we were talking about injured pride. What about honourable pride? Pride in duty? What about Parvateshwar? Think of the first time Shiva saw him. He was uncompromising. Curt. Not even a namaste. Even when Nandi took off Shiva's cravat and displayed his blue neck, Parvateshwar wasn't moved, he merely strained his neck to get a better view. Daksha and Kanakhala were openly in tears; they were ecstatic.

Their ecstasy exasperated Parvateshwar. He was a Suryavanshi, a Meluhan! Their society was based on pure merit. What had this rough-hewn tribal done to deserve the respect of Meluha? Meluha was the source of his pride.'

Gargi: 'Shiva saw him. But did he see Shiva?'

Dharma Raj: 'Oh, he did. Parvateshwar saw everything. It's just that, for him, respect had to be earned. And he would only respect someone for their achievements.'

Gargi: 'Why?'

Dharma Raj walked to the bookshelf and picked up a book. He gazed at the cover and let his fingers glide over the image of Lord Shiva. His back actually, as the Mahadev looked out over Mansarovar Lake.

Dharma Raj turned around. 'Listen to the reason from the warrior's own mouth. "That is the fundamental rule of Lord Ram. Only your karma is important. Not your birth. Not your sex. And certainly not the colour of your throat!"' Dharma Raj walked back to his armchair with the book. 'Of course, Parvateshwar had to earn respect too, and he always did. People like him are toughest on themselves, in their need to earn respect through their conduct. But they also readily give respect when it has been earned.'

Lopamudra: 'The first time he deigned to even speak to Lord Shiva was to describe to him the system that Lord Ram had created to ensure a society in which a person's caste was decided purely by his abilities and merit. His karma. These were the principles on which his Meluha was built. And his pride, too. But it was not an egotistical pride.'

Gargi: 'Why do both of you say that with such certainty?'

Lopamudra: 'Because he was ready to concede a point that was well made against the source of his pride. His ego did not push him to excuse the inexcusable. When Lord Shiva pointed out to Daksha, Kanakhala and Parvateshwar the deceit with which he and his tribe had been administered Somras on entering Meluha, both Kanakhala and Daksha made excuses. They offered mitigating reasons and spoke of gains that had accrued to their tribe. Their apologies were qualified. They had no choice, Daksha said. Kanakhala was apologetic, but pointed out that the tribe was healthier now and was never really at any kind of risk. Only Parvateshwar's apology was unqualified. To him, a lie was an appalling thing. Deception was unacceptable. Period.'

Shiva, the Tibetan leader of a mountain tribe, arrives in Meluha to a resounding welcome that is inexplicable to him, and to one other man: Parvateshwar. The rest, from the highest to the lowest, hail him as their prophesied saviour and lord. But Parvateshwar, the proud Meluhan general, is unmoved. Even abrasive.

Over time, Shiva earns Parvateshwar's attention. Then, his regard. Then, respect. And finally, his devotion and worship.

Shiva and his entourage reach Karachapa, the city of commerce, situated at the confluence of the Indus and the Western Sea. Governor Jhooleshwar organises a *yagna*, a *ceremonial fire sacrifice,* in honour of the Neelkanth. Sati, being a vikarma, decides not to attend the ceremony. She watches it from afar, seated on her balcony in the guesthouse. And yet, Tarak, an immigrant, objects to her presence. It is a technical objection, but Tarak is a troublemaker. He taunts and humiliates Sati till she snaps and invokes the *agnipariksha* duel, a *trial by fire.*

Tarak is a hardy, muscular mountain man, so everyone attempts to dissuade Sati, even Parvateshwar and Brahaspati. But not Shiva. Not only does he readily agree to the duel, he visits her and helps her hone her strategy. He boosts her confidence

and offers training and tactical advice. On the day
of the duel, Sati defeats Tarak. Parvateshwar had
wanted to kill Tarak the previous night, to save his
precious godchild. With his support for her, Shiva
makes inroads into his steely, impenetrable emotions.

As they journey out of Karachapa, they encounter
refugees from the village of Koonj, fleeing from an
ongoing terrorist attack. Parvateshwar is frustrated.
He wants to head to the village with his soldiers,
but he has been told to protect the Neelkanth (the
Blue-throated One, i.e., Shiva) and Princess Sati. He
listens to the horrific tale of the villagers, impotent
with rage. And then he hears Shiva's booming voice.
Shiva exhorts the villagers to return and fight. But the
villagers are hesitant. Shiva then rips off his cravat
and reveals his blue throat to inspire them and the
soldiers. He leads them into battle. Parvateshwar is
energised.

Sati is grievously injured in the battle.
Recovering, she finally embraces her love for Shiva.
Daksha suggests that the vikarma law be amended
to declassify noblewomen who have birthed still-
born children so that Shiva and Sati can marry.
Parvateshwar is appalled at the unfairness of this.
Shiva then scraps the vikarma law in its entirety.

Though Parvateshwar does not approve of laws being changed, he appreciates that this change is fair, and not one that favours only the nobility.

Nachiket: 'His respect for Shiva increased steadily. He thanked him for helping Sati in her *agnipariksha*. His regard spiked as Shiva led the onslaught on the Naga terrorists in the village of Koonj. There was a sharper turning point when Shiva repealed the vikarma law in its entirety, for everyone. Parvateshwar was deeply impressed. Shiva had remained true to one of Ram's fundamental principles: the law applied to everybody. There could be no exceptions.'

Nachiket paused.

Gargi: 'Go on. You're bringing Parvateshwar to life!'

Nachiket: 'Okay. Some detail then. Shiva came up with a brilliant military strategy on the eve of the final battle. Parvateshwar's respect for him deepened. Shiva sent Drapaku at the head of the Vikarma brigade to confront the Chandravanshi detachment to the east. He did not lead himself. Parvateshwar's heart plummeted with disappointment. And then, that moment arrived … It really made my heart sing. Daksha blithely blessed Parvateshwar as he went into battle. The emperor of Meluha then suggested to Shiva that they make their way towards the viewing platform. Shiva turned around and told him that his place was with the soldiers on the battlefield … "There are no bystanders in a *dharmayudh*." Ram's words. And pride melted. It was replaced by devotion. Shiva had finally earned a magnificent follower. Parvateshwar walked up to him and offered a formal military salute. And bowed. As low as he bowed to the image of Ram every morning. Magnificent!'

Nachiket's eyes were moist. Stories of inspirational leadership never failed to move him. He was a budding Parvateshwar himself!

Gargi said gently, 'Honourable pride, yes. Positive pride, yes. But would you call it magnificent pride?'

Nachiket: 'It's magnificent to me. But that might be Sati for you. Also magnificent, I concede.'

Gargi: 'Yes, without doubt! She could have stood for injured pride so easily. But she chose to flip her destiny and become magnificent instead.'

Sati is a Kshatriya warrior, both in spirit and form.

Sati, Daksha and Veerini are out on a picnic on the banks of River Saraswati. Sati is sixteen years old. Parvateshwar, their conscientious bodyguard, accompanies them. Sati wanders off into the forest and comes upon a woman being attacked by a pack of wild dogs. Without a second thought, she roars and jumps into the fray. Daksha and Parvateshwar hear the sound and rush towards it. They find Sati ferociously fighting off the pack, although she is dangerously outnumbered. Parvateshwar and Daksha rush to her assistance, Daksha's parental instinct overcoming his innate cowardice.

Much later, Sati gives birth to a stillborn child, or so she is told. She embraces her vikarma destiny without demur. She withdraws from life and confines herself to the boundaries imposed by fate and an unjust law.

Sati is an uncompromising stoic.

When Shiva enters her life, a fork appears in her pre-destined path. He woos her, but is unsuccessful. Then the Pandit of Mohenjo daro explains to him that Sati has the power to rebel against the vikarma law if she wants to. But she accepts the unfairness of life even as she uses her formidable abilities for the good of society. Shiva finally understands: she craves respect, not protection. The nature of his courtship changes. And the fair maiden melts. They marry.

There's a further softening as the circle of love expands. She discovers that her elder son, Ganesh, is alive. That she has a twin sister, the fiery Kali, queen of the Nagas. Both Kali and Ganesh are Nagas, but Shiva has broadened her simplistic world view. She embraces them with love.

But warrior pride can be insidious. If not carefully navigated, it can even be fatal. When Sati's entourage is informed about a peace conference to be held by Emperor Daksha, Shiva is in the foreign land of Pariha. The invitation to the conference is for him, and not for her. But Sati decides to attend—without the army, which she unilaterally decides will stay back, within the walls of Lothal. Her advisors counsel her against this. Maatali, king of Vaishali, does not mince his words. 'That is most unwise,' he says. Veerbhadra pleads with her not to go.

But she does. And meets her death at the hands of Swuth, the brutal Egyptian assassin.

Dharma Raj: 'I think the trick, especially for a proud person, is to focus on others. Lady Sati did that from her childhood. After she fought off a pack of wild dogs to protect an injured immigrant, Daksha was livid. "Dammit, Sati! Who asked you to be a hero?" he said to her. But nobody asks a hero to be a hero. You just become who you already are, deep inside.'

Lopamudra: 'But, even then, she had her *Pitratulya*, the *one who is like a father*. Parvateshwar told her he was proud of her. That she was a true follower of Lord Ram and that it was the duty of the strong to protect the weak. That was the crucial flip for a person who thrived on pride. To learn to make others proud of her.'

Dharma Raj: 'Yes. But how did that flip happen? When did it get completed? Lady Sati was arrogant in her self-righteousness. She not only insisted on following the law, come what may, she believed that all Meluhans would follow the law. She took pride in the group. Her decision to go to the peace conference was unwise. A thin line divides courage from false bravado, and pride makes a brave person imprudent. She said loftily that she would return with the peace treaty. Just like that! Veerbhadra told her to nominate someone else to attend the conference on her behalf. It was a judicious suggestion, but she refused. Her pride in her group was fully exposed when she insisted that she would only take Suryavanshis with her because they were familiar with Meluhan customs ... as if Shiva's friend, Veerbhadra, lacked the intelligence to adopt Meluhan ways at a time like that.'

Lopamudra: 'Actually, Lady Sati herself was suspicious of her father's bona fides. She said so, to Mayashrenik. "Meluhans may follow the law, Brigadier. My father does not ... " And yet, she put her life at risk. And, as it turned out, the life of her bodyguards, and the loyal Nandi too. That haughty pride could not be subdued.'

Gargi: 'But in the end, what magnificence! The ferocious pride of a lioness! She stands tall, Baba!'

Dharma Raj: 'Yes. Magnificence. When did her pride become magnificent? When she acknowledged her own arrogance. Pride transforms when it observes itself and is replaced by true humility. When pride in oneself is replaced by the pride that others take in you. The flip! Swuth did not at first want to sully his tongue by speaking to a woman. He believed a woman was little better than an animal. He asked Qa'a to torture and kill her. And then he saw her. Really saw her. Beyond her skills as a warrior, he saw her character. Beyond her strength, he saw her sense of honour. Beyond her mortal wounds, he saw her defiance. Beyond her broken body, he saw her unbroken spirit, her invincible human spirit. She became his final kill. His Goddess. Truly magnificent.'

The night air was ornamented by silence.

Nachiket: 'We should be leaving. Don't you have an early morning class, Mrs S?'

Gargi: 'No. Rucha cancelled; she has fallen ill. My first class is at 7.30 a.m. now. And I am not going anywhere till we tackle my favourite character in the No-Mahabharata! And match it with, I don't know, someone from No-Meluha. Or No-Ramayana!'

Nachiket: 'Karna!'

6

LOYALTY IS A SLIPPERY SLOPE

Lopamudra: 'Baba and I almost fought over Karna last week. You're not going to be thrilled to hear his take.'

Gargi: 'I'll give him a good fight, I assure you. If he thinks Karna is anything but magnificent, that is.'

Dharma Raj: 'Hmmm. He is a tantalising character, isn't he?'

Nachiket: 'They all are.'

Dharma Raj: 'No doubt. But in his case, the paradox is stark. Is he "good" or "bad"? Why is this Pandava fighting alongside the Kauravas? Why is his character so tragic? Why is he everyone's favourite? I must admit, I like him too.'

'Could it be because he is all heart?' Gargi said, suddenly all fired up. 'Loyal? Large-hearted? Brave? Famously generous? And was he wronged? Cheated? Denied?'

Dharma Raj: 'Are you talking about Karna or Ganesh, Lord of the People?'

Ganesh, the Lord of the People, is the nephew of Kali, queen of the Nagas. Kali is full of vengeance, anger and hatred. But she loves her nephew. She is even able to find kindness in her heart for this wounded, valiant soul.

Ganesh is wise beyond measure. The Naga royal council relies on his counsel in all matters, soft and hard. When the queen wants to ban sad songs from the land of Panchavati, they vote against her move. Ganesh loves these songs that trigger the powerful emotions he holds tightly within. When the council proposes to stop sending medicines to the Brangas, Ganesh interrupts the proceedings and makes them realise that a substantial proportion of their wealth can be traced to the Brangas. The supply of medicines is but gratitude, not munificence.

For all her strengths, Kali is unable to master the qualities that Ganesh embodies: an unshakeable calm and a sagacious, non-judgemental view of life and of people—except when it comes to his mother, Sati, the princess of Meluha. The lady who abandoned him as a child and mortally wounded his spirit. He stalks her with obsessive determination, looking for answers and redemption.

Gargi laughed. 'It does sound like Ganesh too, I admit. But we are on Karna just now.'

Dharma Raj: 'Try and disconnect from him, Garu. You are not his advocate. That is the nub of it, actually. At some level, we all like to identify with Karna. He symbolises some fractured qualities in us that could well destroy us.'

Gargi: 'Like?'

Dharma Raj: 'Loyalty.'

Nachiket: 'That's too much, Baba. How is loyalty a negative quality? Karna stood by Duryodhana because he was a true friend.'

Gargi: '"Never rat on your friends," Robert De Nero said.'

Dharma Raj: 'He also said, "Always keep your mouth shut!" Huh, kiddo?'

Gargi squealed in mock anger.

Nachiket: 'I would have never got away with saying that to her!'

Lopamudra: 'Baba himself would have pounced on you.'

Nachiket smiled, shook his head and moved on. 'Karna is reminding me of Kumbhakarna now. He too was loyal. So was Dushasana, to Duryodhana!'

Gargi: 'I repeat, Karna. Right now!'

Nachiket: 'All right. Karna was indebted to

Duryodhana, who had made him the king of Anga when all the others had humiliated him and mocked his obvious talent. Duryodhana redeemed the honour of the great warrior. Was he supposed to forget that?'

Gargi: 'I agree with Kit. How is loyalty evil? We must all be loyal, especially to those who have stood by us. It's a positive thing.'

Dharma Raj: 'You must never forget a good turn or a friendly act. But unquestioning loyalty is not a positive thing. Karna stood with Duryodhana to the bitter end. He could not bring himself to question either his friend's actions or his own loyalty, even when it became obvious that Duryodhana was on a slippery slope and fast descending into moral degeneration. Anything that is not constantly examined by our higher intelligence cannot be wholly positive.'

Dharma Raj paused to let his words sink in.

Lopamudra said softly, 'Your baba made me think hard about this, and he's right. Loyalty is an unequal relationship. Justice may be blind, but regard should not be. It must be earned every day. Yes, Duryodhana did a magnanimous thing, but that did not mean he was above criticism for the rest of his life. If you degrade yourself, then people around you have the right to withdraw their loyalty. Karna should have done that.'

Gargi: 'This is upsetting. I'm very fond of him.'

Lopamudra: 'I'm fond of him too. But don't think of Karna as a man. Think of him as a quality.'

Gargi: 'Aaji told me the story of Maharishi Valmiki when I was a child.'

Nachiket: 'Maharishi Valmiki who wrote the Ramayana?'

Lopamudra: 'And the Adbhuta Ramayana. Go on, Gargi. What did she tell you?'

Gargi: 'According to some folk traditions, Valmiki was a highway bandit. To cut a long story short, one day, his wife and child told him that they refused to share the burden of his bad karma. Even though he did what he did for their sake, to take care of them. As far as they were concerned, his banditry was his personal wrong. Valmiki realised then the error of his ways, pursued good karma, and became the great Rishi Valmiki we all know. The refusal of his wife and child to share his bad karma, in effect saying "*Mere naam ka bill mat phaado*", actually did him good.'

Lopamudra laughed. 'That's the kind of thing your father would say. *Not on my account*! Your grandmother was right. We shoulder the consequences of our actions alone.'

Dharma Raj: 'Getting back to Karna, remember one thing. Withdrawing regard is not the same as being disrespectful. When you withdraw your regard, you do not discard civility. Quite the contrary. You must be compassionate and understanding. Human nature plays tricks on all of us, and disrespect only emerges from arrogance and intolerance.'

Nachiket: 'It's so obvious now, but it would never have occurred to me. We play so many roles: spouse, child, parent, friend, colleague, citizen. None of these must pull us away from dharma. Like you said, Baba, the way we *must be*.'

Gargi: 'That's it, then, about Karna? Unquestioning loyalty?'

Dharma Raj: 'There's more to him. But we haven't finished with loyalty yet. What about Kumbhakarna's loyalty to Raavan?'

Nachiket: 'Hmmm … that too is loyalty. What kind of loyalty is that? The loyalty of love?'

Dharma Raj: 'Yes. Kumbhakarna loves his brother and will not take sides with anyone against him. Most of the time, he has no individual agency. He will not do anything his brother has not sanctioned. There is beauty in such loyalty, even if it manifests in a villain. And it's different from the kind of loyalty that's based on fear. That's ugly.'

Raavan is an accomplished smuggler at fifteen.
Successful, efficient, and cruel. Kumbhakarna, on the
other hand, is a gentle and sensitive soul. He resonates
with empathy even as Raavan denudes himself of all
the softer emotions. Except those headed in one
direction: Vedavati.

When Raavan lets Kumbhakarna into his secret
chamber and shows him his paintings of Vedavati,
Kumbhakarna is instantly affected. 'We will find her,
Dada,' he tells his lovelorn brother. Over the next
three years, he is engaged in the greatest karma of
his life, finding and restoring to his brother his only
hope for redemption: Vedavati. It takes him three
years, but he finally locates her in the village of
Todee, near Vaidyanath. He returns home jubilant.

The brothers immediately leave for Todee. On
the way, they stop at the island of Mahua, where
Raavan organises an initiation visit to a courtesan-
house for his virgin brother. Later, as they are about
to board the ship, Kumbhakarna finds a note tied
into a knot at the end of his angavastram. 'Help me.'
He knows immediately that it is from the little girl
who served him alcohol and food at the courtesan-
house. Kumbhakarna cannot ignore her plea. Raavan
is exasperated by his brother's saviour impulse.

Raavan only relies on his ability to exploit, not help. But Kumbhakarna will not budge. Raavan cusses, but relents. They rescue the little girl, Samichi, and Raavan acquires a devotee for life.

Much later, Raavan and Kumbhakarna halt at Kishkindha, on their way to Mithila for Sita's swayamvar. They are welcomed by King Vali, who appears unusually distracted and depressed. His half-brother Sugreev, known for his gambling and drinking ways, has gone missing. Angad, Vali's son and the apple of his eye, is also missing.

Raavan shares the rumours with Kumbhakarna: Queen mother Aruni had revealed to Vali on her deathbed that Angad is the son of Vali's wife, Tara, and his brother Sugreev. According to the tradition of niyog, when a man cannot sire a child, his wife can approach a rishi, who has the social sanction to impregnate her. Vali's mother, however, had chosen to ask Tara to approach her younger son, Sugreev. Angad is Vali's pride and joy, and he is heartbroken to learn that his son carries the blood of his indolent brother. Kumbhakarna is appalled by Aruni's behaviour. 'Why did she do it in the first place? And if she did, why didn't she just remain quiet? How incredibly selfish!'

Raavan sees an opportunity to use this rift between the brothers to wipe out the Vaanar dynasty and bring

Kishkindha under the Lankan yoke. Kumbhakarna, however, only feels Vali's pain.

Kumbhakarna is God-fearing. At Sita's swayamvar, Raavan throws the Pinaka on the table and walks away when Vishwamitra insults him. Kumbhakarna steps up, quickly unstrings Lord Rudra's bow and brings it to his forehead with both hands. He silently apologises to Lord Rudra on his brother's behalf and begs the Lord to not hold it against him. He lays the bow on the table with the greatest respect and dignity, and then briskly follows his seething brother. Raavan too is a devotee of Lord Rudra, but Kumbhakarna is the one who understands and practises true reverence.

Lopamudra: 'Kumbhakarna was simple, yet enigmatic. His brother's pain was his own. And Raavan's was not the only pain he felt. He felt Vali's anguish, little Samichi's desperation.'

Nachiket: 'Kumbhakarna understood love. He promised Raavan that he would seek out the love of his life. And he did! Fulfilling his brother's desires was his mission. His brother's joy was his joy.

'He valued family bonds. He did not like it that his brother did not respect their mother. When Raavan ranted against her, Kumbhakarna rebuked him. He wanted Raavan to bond with their half-siblings, Vibhishan and Shurpanakha. He saw a sister in Shurpanakha while Raavan only saw a tool for his schemes.'

Dharma Raj: 'But Kumbhakarna allowed her to be used as a tool.'

Nachiket: 'Yes. He had surrendered to his loyalty to Raavan. But—as you say, Baba—listen carefully to what comes after the "but" … *but* he had the capacity to venerate and revere the ideal. He revered the Sapt Sindhu. When the brothers landed on the beach of Karachapa with their army, he jumped off the boat and touched the wet sand to his forehead. Then again, Kumbhakarna did not hesitate to ravage the land alongside the brother he idolised.'

Dharma Raj: 'He reminds me of Brutus, most honourable man!'

Lopamudra: 'Ha! That is funny! But seriously, Kumbhakarna is fascinating. God-fearing, reverential. And yet, his hero was Raavan. He craved to emulate him.'

Nachiket: 'But he was also constantly trying to change his brother to make him worth emulating! He never failed to speak truth to Raavan. And then he let it go. I should have listened to you, Raavan always said. But he never did!'

Lopamudra: 'Kumbhakarna saw his brother for what he was. But there are always some blind spots when loyalty is built on deep love.'

His father had told him that 'Raavan' is 'one who roars to frighten people'. Vedavati offers him a correction. 'The root of the word "Raavan" is "Ru"—the "one who roars". But what will you roar for? Will you roar to frighten people? Or will you, like Lord Rudra, roar to shield those who need protection? Roar, noble Raavan. Roar to protect the innocent, the poor, the needy.'

Her words inspire him; he is ripe for transformation. He begins making plans to do good and be good. He writes and seals a hundi for fifty thousand gold coins and gives it to her. He calls it his first act of genuine goodness. Vedavati accepts it and promises to use it for the good of the villagers. Raavan leaves with a spring in his step. Kumbhakarna is thrilled. His prayers have been answered.

Alas, Sukarman, the wastrel son of the landlord, has seen and heard all that transpired between them. And he is very interested in the fifty thousand gold coins.

Kumbhakarna gets wind of the tragedy and drags Sukarman to Raavan. They ride into Todee,

now wrapped in a deathly silence. Vedavati and her
husband Prithvi have been brutally murdered. She lies
in a pool of blood, her face still and serene. Killed
by Sukarman and his thuggish friends for those fifty
thousand gold coins.

Raavan becomes unhinged. Kumbhakarna is in
despair, but he remains by the side of his brother.
Raavan kills Shochikesh, Sukarman's kind-hearted
father. He then orders that every Todee villager be
murdered. No bystander is innocent. And then he
tortures and kills Sukarman, slowly.

Gargi: 'Raavan could have found redemption in
Vedavati. She inspired him to do good and be good. To
discover his inner hero. It's interesting, na? There's a
hero inside a villain and a villain inside a hero!'

Lopamudra smiled. 'Yes! But the bigger redemption
may have been Kumbhakarna's.'

Gargi: 'It's amazing that Kumbhakarna obeyed his
brother regardless of what the command was. He never
stepped back.'

Dharma Raj: 'Inside, though, Kumbhakarna kept
returning to his centre. Again and again. He looked
at the village full of dead people in Todee—brutally

killed by his brother and himself—and felt ashamed. He wanted them to be cremated with respect. When Raavan dismissed his pleas, he vowed that he would atone for it.'

Gargi: 'But he would still not move away from his brother.'

Nachiket: 'And that's the nature of loyalty.'

Prahast, one of Raavan's military commanders, brutally assaults the peaceful Devendrars of Mumbadevi port. The defenders self-immolate en masse rather than suffer defeat and dishonour at the hands of the Lankans. Even some of Prahast's soldiers desert the army, shocked by his brutality. Kumbhakarna is appalled. He begs Raavan to punish Prahast and make an example of him. And Raavan does set an example— but of the deserters. His orders are that they must be caught and publicly executed. Kumbhakarna tells him there is a difference between ruthlessness and adharma, but Raavan does not understand. 'Do it, Kumbha,' he says. And Kumbha, the loyal servant, carries out his brother's orders.

Kumbhakarna now begins to travel. He is escaping, both in search of answers and to take his brother's actions off his mind. He expiates his guilt in whatever way he can—through charity, negotiating bad trade deals (which hurt Lanka and aid its competitors), refusing to accumulate wealth. Then, in Ethiopia, he meets M'Bakur, who teaches him that charity must be given to the worthy. Deliberately negotiating bad trade deals is a waste of money and only benefits the wealthy. 'Help the poor instead,' M'Bakur tells him. 'Help them in the name of your brother. Earn good karma for him.'

Kumbhakarna is enthused. He returns to Sigiriya and reminds his brother of his intention, many years ago, to build a hospital in Vaidyanath in the name of the Kanyakumari. Raavan tells his brother he will burn all his money rather than spend it on the Sapt Sindhu, even if it is for a hospital in Vaidyanath. But Kumbhakarna has his way. He takes Raavan's hand and presses the ring on his forefinger, with the royal seal, on the document authorising the building of the hospital.

Dharma Raj: 'You notice that this simple, beautiful soul became increasingly melancholic. He loved his brother to death. He was compelled to obey him, come what may. But he was increasingly torn between loyalty and dharma. He became a celibate. That was his private

atonement. Kumbhakarna's swadharma was to save
Raavan, and he had to do it to the best of his abilities.'

Gargi: 'I love Kumbhakarna!'

Nachiket: 'More than you love Karna?'

'Be glad it's not more than you!' Gargi stuck out her
tongue at him.

Lopamudra said, as if she had not heard them,
'Kumbhakarna's loyalty was front-foot. His wordless
message to his brother was: "You can do better than
this. At least try." The same message that Vedavati gave
to Raavan.'

Nachiket: 'That's the key difference between
Kumbhakarna and Karna. Karna did not force his way
with Duryodhana even once. Maybe Karna didn't really
love Duryodhana. He just felt indebted.'

Gargi: 'Nor did Duryodhana love Karna the way
Raavan loved Kumbhakarna. True love is a two-way
street. You must have it in you to become a beloved.'

Dharma Raj: 'Aai said that earlier: love needs a
beloved. Anyway, Karna's loyalty was very different. He
was a complex man. Kumbhakarna was simple, gentle
and sensitive. He almost never thought about himself,
such was his loyalty. Again and again, he tried to walk
away from adharma. But he couldn't walk away from
his brother!'

Lopamudra: 'He knew his brother. He also
understood dharma. And yet he was loyal, you see!'

Gargi: 'Beautiful. Can we stop with the loyalty now?'

Dharma Raj: 'Nope! There's disloyalty too. Is it dharmic? Adharmic?'

Gargi: 'Ha! Never a dull moment with this dharma stuff! The nobility of disloyalty!'

Lopamudra: 'It can be both, noble and ignoble. It's always about the context and the intention. Bona fides, as you like to say!' Lopamudra cast a glance at her husband and then looked away. 'So, who reminds us of disloyalty?'

Nachiket: 'You know, I admire Brahaspati a great deal.'

Brahaspati is the chief scientist of the Meluhan empire. He leads the team of scientists that manufactures Somras on Mount Mandar. He is devoted to study and experimentation, trial and analysis. He is most animated when discussing science.

Shiva and Brahaspati strike an instant rapport. Shiva finds it refreshing to be treated as an equal and not as the promised messiah, and his intellect and curiosity appeal to Brahaspati. He enjoys their conversations. They joke. They laugh. At each other and with each other. They develop a bond. Shiva begins to see Brahaspati as a brother. In fact, after Sati, his favourite person.

To love is to trust. Shiva confides in Brahaspati and also reveals his love for Sati. He seeks advice. Brahaspati offers good advice. He helps Shiva understand the reasons behind Sati's hesitation. But reciprocity is not for the scientist. Brahaspati does not tell his friend about having loved and lost Tara. People of the mind struggle with truly trusting even those they love.

After Sati's *agnipariksha* in Karachapa, Brahaspati parts company with Shiva's entourage. As he leaves, he says to Shiva that if there is one person who can suck negativity from this land, it is Shiva. And that he will help him in any way he can. But he does not reveal his devastating plan to Shiva.

Later, he attends Shiva and Sati's wedding, but leaves soon after. He lies to Shiva about a scheduled experiment. He returns to Mount Mandar and destroys it. He fakes his own death. And disappears from Shiva's life. For five years.

Shiva suffers. He is so bitter about the carefully choreographed death of Brahaspati that he rejects his son Ganesh, blaming him for having killed his brother. This creates a seemingly unbridgeable rift between him and his precious Sati. But Shiva cannot forgive

Ganesh for killing Brahaspati, which is the truth as he knows it.

Brahaspati, meanwhile, has allied with the Nagas. He has taken it upon himself to solve the Somras problem of the empire, the Neelkanth notwithstanding. For five years, he perseveres. Only when he fails does he accept that it's time to join the Shiva brigade again.

Years later, Brahaspati reveals himself to Shiva. When it suits him. And pays the price for disloyalty. 'My mission has gained a leader, but I have lost a friend,' he says to Nandi and Parshuram.

Dharma Raj: 'Yes, Brahaspati was disloyal. To both Lord Shiva and Meluha.'

Nachiket: 'How was he disloyal to Shiva? He aligned with him eventually, didn't he?'

Lopamudra: 'That wasn't loyalty but inevitability. He revealed himself to Lord Shiva when it suited him. I'm not judging it, Raj!' Lopamudra raised her hands in defence as she saw her husband's eyebrows rise. 'Brahaspati believed in knowledge and science. "Knowledge is a capable but cold-hearted master," isn't that what he said? He was loyal to no one. He was more mind, less heart.'

Nachiket: 'It's hard to commend disloyalty, however noble the intentions behind it may be. Loyalty, trust, faith … these are beautiful concepts, and they are also stepping-stones to humility and gratitude. Loyalty is a heart thing.'

Dharma Raj: 'That it is. A heart thing. And Brahaspati is pure mind over heart. He misled Lord Shiva and led him to believe that he had died in the explosions on Mount Mandar. For five years, he kept the truth from Lord Shiva. His buddy, his brother!'

Gargi: 'He had good intentions.'

Dharma Raj: 'Yes, but do you think there's also a bit of egotism in his actions? Along with rationality and sense, of course. Intentions need careful unwrapping. There's no doubt that Brahaspati too was an honourable man!'

Lopamudra: 'Haha! There comes Brutus again! But I understand what you mean. He believed he could spare Lord Shiva the dreadful personal fate of the Mahadevs. Spare the Mahadev from the destiny of being the Mahadev! He took it upon himself to destroy evil. And he really believed that he was doing it for both Meluha and his friend. Oh yes, that's egotism all right.'

Gargi: 'But he may only have wanted to protect his friend. He loved Shiva.'

Dharma Raj: 'Oh, absolutely. That is true. He did it

to protect his friend. I am only questioning the "only". Very few actions have just one underlying motive. We like to think so, and acknowledge only the best motive, even to ourselves—the one that suits our image of our self and what we want to project. There is a reason why our unconscious is called the unconscious. It takes an amazing amount of courage to confront the self underneath the layers that our ego builds up. Face the face! You said that once, Lopa.'

Lopamudra was looking at her husband, her eyes alive with love and admiration.

Nachiket picked up the thread. 'Under the cover lie other motives. Yes, Brahaspati wanted to protect his friend. *And* protect his self-image.'

Dharma Raj: 'Years later, he told Lord Shiva he trusted him but not those around him. He was waiting for him to part ways with them. But Lord Shiva called his bluff. He told him point-blank that he was only here now because he had been unable to accomplish the mission on his own. Brahaspati was honest enough then, to admit that he needed to meet Lord Shiva because he had failed.'

Nachiket: 'You mention trust. That's also a heart thing. "Trust but verify" is not trust. It may make eminent sense in a given situation, but it's not real trust. A toddler trusts her parents. She will leap without hesitating. She trusts. Makes you smile, na? Trust is beautiful.'

Gargi: 'But Brahaspati was all head because he had suppressed his heart. He had lost his love, Tara, to other people's machinations. Love may have softened him, given the opportunity. Anyway, Parvateshwar was also disloyal, wasn't he? To Shiva, his living God!'

When Parvateshwar discovers what havoc the Somras has wreaked upon the Nagas and the Brangas, he is ashamed. Lost and unsure, for the first time in his life. His emperor's actions have put him in a situation in which his God, the Neelkanth, might declare a war on his motherland. Which side should he pick?

He is inspired by Shiva, but is honour-bound to protect Meluha. He stopped using the Somras the day he discovered it was evil. But he will die defending the land that manufactures the Somras.

'Shreyaan sva dharmo vigunaha para dharmaat svanushthitat,' Parvateshwar tells Ayurvati. It is better to make mistakes on the path of swadharma than to live the perfect life on a path that belongs to another.

He begins to stay away from his companions' strategy discussions. He walks away even from his wife and brother-in-law when the Neelkanth's plans for Meluha are being discussed. When he meets Rishi Bhrigu from the Meluhan camp, he staunchly defends Shiva, whom Bhrigu calls a fraud. Bhrigu asks him to leave Shiva and come to Meluha. 'I cannot leave without taking my Lord's permission,' he responds.

When Parvateshwar is eventually imprisoned by Kali, he stoically awaits the arrival of Shiva. Shiva arrives, and is enraged. How could his Parvateshwar choose to fight him? Parvateshwar tells him he has no choice.

'Swadharma nidhanam shreyaha para dharmo bhayaavahah,' he says to Shiva. *Death in the course of doing one's swadharma is better than following another's path, for that is truly dangerous.*

Shiva lets him go and says to him, 'The next time we meet, it will be on the battlefield. And that will be the day I kill you.' Parvateshwar looks at Shiva and replies, 'That will also be the day of my liberation, my Lord.'

Lopamudra: 'Parvateshwar was inspired by Lord Shiva, but his loyalty lay with Meluha. Always. He believed in the destruction of evil. In fact, he stopped having Somras when he realised what it had done to the Nagas, the Brangas, and to Mother Nature. But he *could not* abandon Meluha. Again, that's the nature of loyalty.'

Nachiket: 'Yes. Ayurvati asked him why he wanted to defend this *halahal* and he told her he was not defending Somras, the *poison*. He was defending Meluha. When Ayurvati said, "They are on the same side," he retorted, "That is my misfortune."'

Lopamudra: 'And yet, he did not leave for Meluha without his Lord's permission. No subterfuge for this man. His duty lay with Meluha, his heart with Lord Shiva. He was loyal to two opposing sides!'

Nachiket: 'Ha. That's true. He was prepared to face death if Shiva decided to punish him, but he would not leave on the sly. It would have been better for his precious Meluha had he just left, without leaving it to chance. But he wouldn't. Really, like you say, Baba, bona fides are everything. What transpires is not in our hands. Whatever will be, will be. All that we control is our inner alignment.'

Gargi: 'What about Nandi?'

Dharma Raj: 'The Meluhan Major ... first Captain, then Major. Nandi represents the simplicity of loyalty. He had no choice. Just like Parvateshwar had no choice. Nandi lived for the Neelkanth; he would die for the Neelkanth. If that meant he had to oppose his country, so be it!'

Nachiket: 'Parvateshwar was at peace with Nandi's choice.'

Gargi: 'Nandi was at peace with Nandi! But he was not at peace with Parvateshwar's choice. In his simple mind, Parvateshwar was wrong. But Parvateshwar had acquired more depth by now. Anandmayi had deepened him.'

Nachiket: 'It's the other way around. Parvateshwar gave depth to Anandmayi. Anandmayi expanded his mind, broadened it. She taught him the truth of multiple truths. The opposite of right is wrong ... simplistic. The opposite of right is left! The rest is context.'

Dharma Raj: 'Anandmayi. Heart over mind. She was loyal to Parvateshwar.'

Parvateshwar discovers that Emperor Daksha has repeatedly broken the law. He has even broken Lord Rudra's law by firing the *daivi astra*. He tells his wife, Anandmayi, that he is confused. 'How do I know which side to pick?' Anandmayi is worried for him, but she is clear. 'Whatever happens, we must have faith in the Neelkanth.' Her husband should stick to his God, she tells him.

A few days later, Parvateshwar and Anandmayi ride out on their favourite steeds. He leans towards her and takes her hand. He tells her that if it comes to war, he will have no choice but to fight on the side of Meluha. Anandmayi tells him that she will then be left with no choice but to oppose him. 'What do we do now?' he asks her. 'Keep riding together ... till our paths allow us,' she says. Her mind knows she will stand by her God, Lord Shiva.

However, when Kali imprisons Parvateshwar, shackling his hands and legs out of an abundance of caution, Anandmayi's heart establishes its dominance over her mind. 'I don't care if the entire world turns against him. I don't even care if the Neelkanth turns against him. I will stand by my husband. He is a good man ... a good man!'

Later, Shiva lets Parvateshwar go, and the Meluhan general makes his lonely way to the harbour, his face impassive, his heart beset by a raging storm. He finds Anandmayi standing by the ship that will take him away from her. Parvateshwar steps forward and embraces her. 'I will miss you. You are the best thing that ever happened to me,' he says. His wife saucily replies, 'And I will continue to happen to you. Let's go.'

'Where?' he asks, bewildered.

'Meluha,' she replies.

Lopamudra: 'I like her. Underneath all that fluff and scatter, she was unshakeable, like a sturdy pillar. She truly believed she would not leave her living God, Lord Shiva. But then her husband was imprisoned, and everything became different. Her heart always knew what her mind did not know. That she would stand by her husband, come what may. When the time came, she knew that her place was beside him.'

Dharma Raj: 'We do not know how we will behave in a crisis until it is upon us. We may think we know, but we don't. When we are truly tested, our deepest, hidden self emerges: beautiful or ugly; strong or weak; hard or soft; steady or escapist; brave or cowardly; envious or unenvious; loving or unloving; benign or malignant. Until then, it is all theory. It is only that moment in which we discover who we really are. And it leaves us either ashamed or proud in its wake.'

Gargi: 'Okay, so whose loyalty is the most beautiful loyalty?'

Lopamudra: 'Kumbhakarna. Kumbhakarna's loyalty is all heart.'

Gargi: 'Anandmayi's too.'

Lopamudra: 'Being loyal was easy for her. Parvateshwar's character made it easy. Had Parvateshwar been a dishonourable man, her mind may have challenged her heart, and it would have been interesting to see what she did then. That would have been her true test. Kumbhakarna was intelligent, and he did not delude himself. He acknowledged Raavan's adharma and his descent. He battled with his conscience. But his heart always knew. Standing by his brother was his life's purpose.'

Nachiket: 'Karna and Kumbhakarna were loyal to adharma. How would you distinguish between them?'

Dharma Raj: 'Karna did not show Duryodhana the mirror. Kumbhakarna never missed an opportunity to show Raavan the mirror. He proved that it was possible to be loyal to both adharma and truth at the same time. Once again, loyal to two opposing sides!'

Nachiket: 'Okay. So who's worth emulating?'

Dharma Raj: 'All of them! They were great men and women. Find your own fit. And try and avoid the sort of loyalty that says, "come-what-may, I'll be loyal."'

Lopamudra: '*Ati sarvatra varjayet. Excess of anything should be avoided.* Extremism in any form is not good.'

7

THE PRICE OF
ANGER

Nachiket's phone began to vibrate. Anirban. 'You're going to live long, chief,' he said, stepping out of the room.

Gargi: 'He's a lovely man, Anirban. You guys should meet Valli too. Malivalaya.'

Lopamudra: 'That's an interesting name.'

Gargi: 'It's Thai for "climbing jasmine". She's a fantastic cook. She also writes beautiful poetry.'

Nachiket returned. 'Anirban and Valli are off to Bandhavgarh. Do you want to go?'

Gargi: 'Isn't it too hot right now?'

Nachiket: 'That's when you see the tigers, my good woman!'

Gargi: 'Hmmm. Let me think … Do we have to let them know right away?'

Nachiket: 'No. I can call him back tomorrow.'

Gargi: 'Great.'

She turned to her father. 'So, Baba, you said there's more on Karna. Like what?'

Dharma Raj: 'Victimhood. An injured nursing of victimhood, actually.'

'That's really unfair, Baba,' Nachiket said as he sat back again. 'Wasn't he entitled to his pain and hurt? He felt abandoned, and the truth is, he *was* abandoned by his mother. He hankered for recognition. And he *was* remarkably talented.'

Gargi: 'And hard-working.'

Nachiket: 'Yes! He felt life didn't give him his due.'

Dharma Raj: 'Entitled to pain and hurt? Interesting. Lord Ganesh too was abandoned by his mother. He did not abandon dharma in return. Far from it. He was remarkably talented, but no, he did not hanker for recognition. You may feel entitled to suffering, but all you're doing is working against yourself.'

Gargi: 'How so?'

Dharma Raj: 'You harm yourself physically and emotionally. You collect debris. Look at Lady Kali. She was also abandoned. If victimhood led to a sense of injury in Karna's case, in her it led to anger. She did not feel like a victim at all, but she was. And it made her angry.'

Kali is Sati's twin sister and the other daughter of Emperor Daksha and Queen Veerini. Born a Naga, she was abandoned by her parents. The existence of Kali and Ganesh, Sati's son, was hidden from Sati. She had been told that her child was stillborn.

Kali may have been denied the status of a princess of Meluha, but she became queen of the Nagas in Panchavati. Years later, Sati meets her in Icchawar: a fierce, jet-black Naga replica of herself. Sati is dumbstruck. All Kali wants to do is kill. 'Kill her!' she screeches to Ganesh. It is the only way her nephew will find peace, she is convinced.

Ganesh is the only one Kali loves and nurtures. But, deep down, she craves affection and acceptance. When Sati asks them to accompany her to Kashi, she readily accepts. She admits she was wrong about her sister. She meets Shiva and wonders if things would have been different had fate blessed her with a husband like Shiva. Maybe, like her sister, the poison could have been sucked out of her life as well.

Both Kali and Ganesh are victims of circumstances, but Kali craves confrontation. Ganesh, on the other hand, seeks to protect and restore. When Kali finally confronts her father in Kashi, Daksha calls her and Ganesh vile. Scum. Kali wants to kill him, but for once, it is her sister, Sati, who draws her sword and almost kills her father. She is brought to her senses by Shiva. Sati says to her father what would have been expected from her twin: 'GET OUT!'

Kali has no need for finer emotions like trust. When she needs to shepherd Shiva's entourage to her fortress, Panchavati, she chooses a circuitous route that will take them a year. She trusts Shiva. But ...

Kali seeks vengeance. 'Obviously, victims will nurse hatred in their hearts,' she says. She wants to destroy Meluha and not just the Somras that has so grievously harmed the Nagas and the Brangas. Ganesh feels no need for vengeance. He does not hand out blame. He does not seek justice either. To him, justice exists for the good of the universe. To maintain the balance and not to settle scores or ignite hatred among human beings. The universe will deliver justice when the time is right. In this life or the next.

Anger invariably extracts a terrible price. News of the Meluhan navy sailing down the river Narmada makes Kali jump to the conclusion that the route to Panchavati has been discovered. She instantly turns on Sati. She screams and shouts, raves and rants. She blames Shiva and Sati's misplaced sense of honour for Parvateshwar still being alive; they should have killed him when they could have. She decides to leave for Panchavati with her fifty ships and all the Naga warriors. She gives her sister a withering look and turns her back on her. 'My people will not suffer for your addiction to moral glory, didi' are her last words to her stranded sister. Later, when Sati dies, Kali is filled with everlasting remorse.

Lopamudra: 'Lady Kali did not *admit* to being a victim, but the little girl inside her felt it very deeply. That's why she was so angry.'

Gargi: 'How can I not feel what I'm feeling?'

Dharma Raj: 'I'm not suggesting you try and not feel what you're feeling. It is disastrous to suppress one's feelings. Respect your feelings, but do not identify with them completely. Use them like the tools they can be. And to use them like tools, you must first learn to be aware of them. Channel their flow with wisdom and awareness. Be the master of your feelings; do not let them control you. Then you will be like Lord Ganesh and not Lady Kali.'

Gargi: 'Kali was not just angry. She was a raging forest fire. She was angry about everything. Meluha was vile, her father was a repulsive goat, Sati was entitled …

Daddy's spoilt little girl, she called her. To her face. The little girl in Kali probably wanted to be Daddy's pet, even if her father was a goat!'

Lopamudra: 'She resented Sati's good fortune. She knew her sister did not know the truth about the existence of Kali and Ganesh, but it made no difference to her. Sense does not penetrate anger. And yes, Kali was beyond angry. She was furious and resentful. Disgusted with the world.'

Nachiket: 'Except her Panchavati …'

Lopamudra: 'Yes, except Panchavati. Because she had fused her idea of herself with Panchavati. Unresolved, deep-seated victimhood can lead to terrible fury. It burns you. She was also quick to condemn. Her first response was attack.'

Nachiket: 'Her second response was attack. Her last response was also attack!'

Nachiket cast a glance at his wife. Her eyes flashed. He laughed, and then she laughed too.

Nachiket continued, his eyes gleaming mischievously, 'Kali came alive in battle. Cold smile, curled lips, glittering eyes, blood-curdling screams … she was in her element! She *had* to be the victor. And, in victory, there could be no mercy. She gave no quarter. There was no strategy, even. Just devastation and maximum damage. Left to herself, she would have wreaked havoc.'

Gargi: 'Ganesh kept her in check. He was also a victim, but he responded so differently ... What would you call the Ganesh response to being victimised?'

Nachiket: 'He flipped it. He was the magnificent one. But Kali first?'

Gargi: 'Okay. Go on about Kali then. I'll tell you one thing. I am not the only one who gets angry. Your anger is the magnificent one! Mine is harmless, it fizzles out. You've said so yourself. It's just that everyone sees my anger. Very few people see yours.'

Nachiket: 'True, *baiko*. But if you get irritated with every rub, how will you shine?'

Dharma Raj smiled.

Gargi: 'Okay, okay. Kali ...'

Lopamudra: 'Garu, if nobody sees his anger, that means he has better self-control. And that's the first step to overcoming it. Don't let the anger control you. You control it. And don't stop there. Many people make that mistake. So long as it's hiding inside, they let it be. That's when the problems begin.' Lopamudra looked at her son-in-law.

Nachiket responded to the look. 'That's true, Ma. If you just keep it inside and don't let anyone see it, it can drive you crazy. You handle the world better, but damage yourself inside. Better the Gargi route then. *Aane do jaane do!* Let it out. It may annoy others, but at least you won't fall ill with it!'

Gargi: 'So okay, my anger is gone! Kali now. She wanted victory, the right way or the wrong way. Subterfuge was fine. Brutality was fine. Whatever it took. She would have killed Parvateshwar, honour be damned!'

Nachiket: 'For Ganesh, however, the right way was everything. And kindness was the right way. All right, all right, let's continue with Kali ...'

Gargi smiled.

Dharma Raj took over. 'Our experience is our reality. Our emotions are our reality. Lady Kali understood dominance, but she also understood fear. Those who know how to frighten others know fear most intimately. Deep inside, she was a frightened little girl, and fearful people are prone to panic. They jump to conclusions.'

Gargi: 'Kali and panic?'

Dharma Raj: 'Of course. When Panchavati was seemingly threatened, she panicked. Frightened and angry people look to blame someone when things go wrong. So did Lady Kali. She instantly blamed Lady Sati and her absent husband. It was Lord Shiva's fault for having let Parvateshwar go. When Lady Sati approached her, she turned her back on her sister. That was the last time she would be with her sister.'

Gargi's eyes glistened with sudden tears.

Dharma Raj: 'Anger can lead to wrong decision-making. It makes you blind. Kali was left with great regret. Great guilt. These are the children of rage, never mind if it's justifiable. They never leave you, these children. They consume you. They kill you every day.'

Gargi: 'Unfortunately, her response to even this terrible guilt was the same: uncontrollable rage. She just wanted to kill …'

Nachiket: 'Rage is like a rabid dog that does not let go.'

The elderly couple watched and listened quietly. They had made their own troubled journey through the ravages of anger. They had made it to the other side.

Gargi: 'You called the Ganesh response magnificent. The flip …'

Nachiket: 'Ganesh was also angry. He wanted to kidnap Sati, remember? He shadowed her obsessively … stalked her. But his anger was controlled. Even his outbursts were of anger, not rage.'

Dharma Raj: 'He bled it out. He cried easily and let it flow. Rage simmers. It doesn't dissipate. You must ride the wave of your emotions, especially anger. They must be expressed. It is the only way to understand yourself.'

And others, his wife thought. She sat as still as a meditative breath.

The younger couple continued their probing.

Gargi: 'Also, Ganesh's anger was looking for answers. He wanted resolution. Completion.'

Nachiket: 'Actually, more than being angry, Ganesh was sad. Melancholic. His expressionless eyes hid immense pain. Maybe there was self-pity. Maybe he felt alone, at least sometimes.'

Gargi: 'You are making him sound like Karna.'

Nachiket: 'Maybe. It's an assembly of victims! But Ganesh's response was very different. He also cried. He cried when he was angry. He cried when he was sad.'

Gargi: 'Tears are for the weak. Was Ganesh weak?'

Lopamudra took a deep breath. 'Tears have nothing to do with strength and weakness. They are a tool given to us by nature. Do you know that the samurai and the medieval knights of Europe were given to tears? They cried when they encountered beauty, courage, nobility … It was a part of their code of conduct—when to cry, how to cry, in whose presence to cry, and when not to cry. Interesting, isn't it? The important thing is, what are you using the tears for? To sink into despair? To manipulate? Control? Divert? For relief or release? To bond? A tool must be used appropriately, but most importantly, it must be used. If emotions are denied or suppressed, they turn toxic. Lord Ganesh cried, but he was courageous and strong. He cried—*and* he was courageous and strong.'

Gargi: 'Hmmm. I love what you just said, Ma.'

Lopamudra smiled.

Nachiket: 'Kali and Ganesh responded very differently to being victims. He acknowledged his hurt. He could trust others. But Kali did not trust anyone. Her "trust" failed at the first test, with Parvateshwar, Shiva, even Sati. Anger hardens the heart, and a hardened heart cannot trust. It only understands suspicion.'

Lopamudra said quietly, as though talking to herself, 'Lord Ganesh's anger did not putrefy into hatred. His pain made him kind. That is the flip you were talking about, Ketu. "I give what I did not receive. I will never tire of giving what I did not receive."' Her voice cracked. Dharma Raj sat still, like the Sphynx.

She continued, 'Whenever possible, Lord Ganesh helped. He rescued Parshuram, and helped him with medicines. He saved the women in the river from the crocodile. Far from being grateful, one of them was cruel and hurtful towards him. But he had no regrets. He saved the tribal woman and her young boy from Prince Ugrasen and his soldiers in the Magadhan forests. They were taking the boy away for bull-racing. Again and again, he risked his life for others. He saved his mother, in Icchawar, from the liger and its lionesses. Later, he protected his brother Kartik from the same creatures. He almost lost his life then. Horribly injured, he prepared for his impending death by sitting back against the hollow in the tree that protected his brother …' Lopamudra choked. Tears rolled down her cheeks.

Dharma Raj stirred. 'They would get to his brother over his dead body. Literally …' His voice trailed away.

Nachiket did not look at his father-in-law. He would not embarrass him. Gargi did not understand what had just happened. But she embraced her father with her eyes.

Lopamudra continued with a tremble in her voice, as if she were talking about someone she knew intimately, 'Lord Ganesh was a man of gold. He was generous, kind-hearted, and full of gratitude. He lived wholeheartedly and whole-mindedly …'

Nachiket took over. 'Yes, Ma. He was grateful to the Brangas for the gold. He asked the Branga king to send gold coins embossed with the image of the king and his kingdom, and not plain gold ingots, so that the Nagas would be constantly reminded of their generous benefactor. He wanted his people to be grateful. But his message to them was subtle, not expressed in words. Words are the least powerful medium of communication!'

Gargi: 'Okay … So we are talking about victims and we began with Karna. And Karna was also generous, Kit.'

Lopamudra: 'That's true. Karna was magnificent too, Garu. He was a lot like Lord Ganesh. But there is a difference. Karna blamed others. Lord Ganesh did not. Karna sank into misery. Lord Ganesh did not. He always swam back to the surface.'

Dharma Raj: 'Lord Ganesh was wracked with guilt, though, when his mother died. He had left her and gone to Panchavati with Lady Kali on a wild goose chase. He abandoned his mother in her final hour of need. He understood only too well the devastation of abandonment. And so he lost his balance.'

Lopamudra looked at her husband and said softly, 'Losing your balance when your mother dies, in such a brutal manner, is not losing your balance. It is an extreme moment.'

Dharma Raj's eyes rested on his wife's face for an eternity. 'True. He returned to equanimity in time.'

Lopamudra's eyes transformed. They began to dance. 'Even earlier, when he was angry, he was composed! His body communicated anger, but his eyes were always quiet. Ultimately, he became the epitome of wisdom. Lord Ganesh, the stoic philosopher!'

Dharma Raj laughed and nodded at his wife. As if in gratitude. 'I just thought of Victor Frankl. Have you heard of him?'

'No,' the chorus rang out.

'Anirban would have known,' Gargi teased her husband.

Dharma Raj: 'He was a renowned psychiatrist. Viktor Frankl, not Anirban ...'

Viktor Frankl is a Jew who lives in Vienna, Austria, in the early 1940s. He is an accomplished neurologist and psychiatrist. The Nazis occupy Austria in 1938, and in 1942, he and his family are picked up and sent to a series of concentration camps. His mother and brother die at Auschwitz. His wife dies at Bergen-Belsen. He himself is put to work laying railway tracks.

Viktor survives. After the war, he returns to Vienna and resumes his psychiatric practice. He marries again. He pioneers a new therapeutic technique called logotherapy. Among his most famous works is *Man's Search for Meaning*.

He heals. He moves on.

Dharma Raj: 'Do you think Frankl had a right to self-pity? If not him, then who? He did not deserve it, but this was what life had handed him. He realised one thing, though: his response to life was in his own hands.'

Dharma Raj paused. No one uttered a sound.

Dharma Raj: 'Every moment, he knew that he could end up in a gas chamber. Seeking meaning from external life became futile. So he turned within and remained "unbitter".'

Nachiket: 'What quality in Frankl set him apart from Karna? Or should I say, who within him?'

Lopamudra: 'His Arjunic qualities. They "kill" the sense of injured victimhood.'

'And what are these qualities?' Gargi asked aggressively.

Lopamudra smiled. 'You don't like Arjuna.'

Gargi shrugged. 'I don't dislike him either.'

Lopamudra: 'That's just it. Arjuna does not excite. But he is the Karmayogi, the one that Krishna "awakens". Any one of us could be that brave disciple.'

Gargi: 'Why did Krishna pick Arjuna? Why did he not pick someone else? Yudhishtra? Bhima? Why not Nakul the Beautiful?'

Lopamudra: 'Arjuna picked Krishna. Krishna was there to be picked. He did not choose anyone. Duryodhana could have picked him, had he wanted to. The disciple comes to the guru.'

Gargi shrugged again. 'I can tell you it's very different today! I'm the one who goes around canvassing for disciples.'

Lopamudra laughed. 'You don't have disciples, Garu. You have students. You are not a guru. You teach yogic postures and breathing techniques. It's not your fault. Very few people have either the time or the patience to learn real yoga. Much less practise it.'

Gargi: 'Hmmm. You can be very deflating, Ma! Back to the disciple then!'

Lopamudra: '"Arjuna" kills "Karna". So, what can victimhood be replaced by?'

Nachiket: 'The ability to question intelligently and separate the outside reality from personal narratives. The disciple-like commitment to dharma above all else.'

Dharma Raj: 'It includes the courage to question even God. There is no place for hesitation, for pre-conceived notions. Arjuna had the audacity to lay down his arms on the battlefield and ask Lord Krishna: "Why should I kill? That too, my own?"'

Lopamudra: 'But remember two things: as you said, Ketu, question intelligently. Ask the question because you are seeking an answer, and not because you want to sound smart or trip up the person you are questioning. And, once you are convinced by the answer, cast away all doubts. Doubts should trigger questioning and not insecurities and passivity. Answers bring clarity and resolve. The Karmayogi has total resolve in his pursuit of dharma.'

Nachiket: 'And what about the lingering feeling of injured victimhood? What can destroy that?'

Dharma Raj: 'Gratitude. Arjuna was repeatedly made aware that he had received more than he deserved from life.'

Ekalavya is the son of the Nishada king. He aspires to be the student of the great Dronacharya. He approaches the great teacher and asks to be taught archery. But Drona turns him down.

Ekalavya is determined. He sculpts an image of his chosen guru in a forest clearing, takes its blessings, and teaches himself the art of archery. One day, the sound of a barking dog disturbs his practice. Ekalavya targets the sound and releases a series of arrows, gagging the animal. On spotting the dog, Drona and his students set out in search of this supreme archer.

They find Ekalavya in the clearing. Drona is amazed at the boy's skill. He asks him, 'Who is your guru?' Ekalavya replies, 'You, Guruji.' Drona looks at his image, and then at Arjuna, standing by his side: the student whom, he has sworn, he will make the greatest archer in the world. He then turns to Ekalavya and demands *guru dakshina*.

Ekalavya replies, 'Anything.'

And the guru coldly asks for his right thumb. Ekalavya draws his knife, chops off his thumb, and places it at the feet of his "guru". Arjuna stands mute, shaken to the bone ...

Karna and Arjuna confront each other on the battlefield on the seventeenth day of the Great War. Arjuna shoots an arrow that pushes Karna's chariot back by a hundred yards. Karna shoots an arrow, and it pushes Arjuna's chariot back by ten yards. As it does, Krishna exclaims '*Waah*!' He cannot hold back his appreciation. It happens again. And Krishna is fulsome in his praise. Again.

Arjuna is offended. He demands to know why Krishna praises Karna, and not Arjuna, when the arrows shot by him have a greater impact. Krishna then makes it obvious to Arjuna that, in Karna, they face a superior warrior. For Arjuna's chariot is steered by the Lord himself, and Lord Hanuman flies on his pennant, lending his strength to them. Karna fights alone. The superior warrior deserves acknowledgement.

Gargi: 'Aaji told me the story of Ekalavya when I was a child. I only thought about Ekalavya at the time. How unfair they were to him. But now I remember something else she said, about Arjuna, the child who stood beside Dronacharya and watched it all happen. "Imagine how burdened Arjuna's conscience was as he stood there. Because he knew that this was done to maintain his supremacy as an archer."'

Nachiket: 'As for Drona, what better example can there be of the dangers of pursuing self-glory? He was full of pride. It was unacceptable to him that an archer could have achieved excellence without his personal guidance.'

Gargi: 'And what about Ekalavya? I remember thinking that he should have refused to make the sacrifice. Why honour an undeserving guru?'

Lopamudra: 'We would not still be talking about him then, the way we are. Ekalavya is a shining example of the possibilities of human diligence and single-mindedness. He is glorious in his astounding act of humility. The best that a man can be. It does not matter what other people are like. The only thing that really matters is what you think of yourself. Not in words expressed to others, but inside you, and honestly. Uncover yourself, at least to yourself!'

Dharma Raj: 'Let us return to the ideas of victimhood and gratitude. You see, we can always find good reasons to convince ourselves that life has cheated us. Karna. Lady Kali. Lord Ganesh. Even Arjuna. But we have also received, at some point, something good from life that we did not deserve. The universe does not favour only a few. We have been given a glass half empty but also half full. Which part do we want to internalise? It's up to us.'

Nachiket: 'Will our inner Karna conquer our Arjuna or will we allow Arjuna to slay the Karna we are so attached to?'

Dharma Raj: 'The answer lies in the mode of death. Again ...'

Lopamudra: 'As we all know, Karna's chariot wheel sank into the soft mud on the battlefield. He stepped down and tried to dislodge it ... You see? Victimhood must descend from its perch and begin to push the wheel of consciousness—as well as resist the temptation to wallow in the soft mud of self-pity. At this point, Arjuna, i.e., gratitude, annihilates Karna, i.e., the anxiety of deprivation and injury. With the aid of Krishna, divine wisdom.'

Nachiket: 'Wow!'

They sat in silence for a while, each lost in self-reflection.

Nachiket: 'Gargi, we must leave.'

Lopamudra: 'Your first session is at 7.30 a.m. now, isn't it? Stay back. You can give us a class here. I would love to do *Pranayama* with you in the morning.'

8

THE PRESENT IS WHAT MATTERS

Gargi was up at five in the morning. So was her father. They sat on the swing and caught up with the news, chai in hand. Gargi, the yoga instructor; Dharma Raj, the doting father.

Half an hour later, Dharma Raj went inside to wake his wife and son-in-law. Gargi laid out the yoga mats. One below the neem tree, the other three facing it.

The others emerged from the house and walked into the garden. They settled down on the mats in *Sukhasana*.

Gargi: 'It's nice to have you with us this time, Kit.'

Nachiket: 'Before we start, why don't you tell us the theory of *Pranayama*?'

Lopamudra: 'I would love that.'

Gargi: 'Okay. But let me know when you want me to stop. I could go on and on!'

Dharma Raj: 'I wouldn't complain!'

Gargi folded her hands and bowed to him with a smile. She said, 'In recent times, modern science has been unwittingly moving in the same direction as the ancient Indian yogis. Physicists say that all matter is energy.

Vibration. The ancients called this energy *Prana*, the *life force*. *Pranayama* is the yogic practice of "drawing out the life force" through breath control. These are breathing exercises that calm the mind and serve as a prelude to advanced yoga and meditation.'

Lopamudra: 'Yesterday, we were discussing self-discovery and self-regulation. Self-regulation begins with breath-regulation; self-observation begins with breath-observation.'

Gargi: 'You're right, Aai. There's a connection between breathing patterns and physiology, between the way we breathe and our thoughts and emotions. Notice the change in your breathing when you are excited, angry, afraid or happy. Notice. That's the keyword. Don't try and control, just notice. *Pranayama* can help us observe our own psychological reality. If we learn to observe our thoughts, we can check them, redirect them, silence them.'

Dharma Raj: 'With increased awareness, we can even reach that inner battlefield we spoke of earlier—Kurukshetra. There, the hero can engage with his inner Kauravas.'

Gargi: '*Pranayama* is too vast a subject. Let's just skim the surface first. Like I said, there's a close relationship between breathing and emotion. Overall, there is a subtle emphasis on breathing in when we are afraid, angry, envious or tempted ... any strong feeling. The emphasis shifts to breathing out when we are in an expressive state and trying to influence our environment.

'By observing ourselves, we can balance the rate of inhalation and exhalation. If the exhalation is more prolonged, ask yourself if you are able to express yourself strongly but are not sensitive to your own feelings and to the feelings of others. You could be hurting inside. Or hurting others, with or without meaning to.

'If you have a long inhalation and a short exhalation, ask yourself if you find it difficult to express how you feel or say the things you want to say. Do you sometimes feel that your life is not in your control? Or that you do not matter to people around you? Do you find it difficult to get things done?

'Observe your breathing and its connection to your emotional experiences.'

Gargi stopped speaking. They closed their eyes and breathed.

Five minutes later, Gargi spoke again, her eyes still closed.

'*Pranayama* begins as an exercise in attention. Don't force yourself. Don't try and control your thoughts or banish them. Just *notice*. Notice the cool air you breathe in, the warm air you breathe out. Notice the sound of the air as it passes through your nostrils. Notice your chest expand and collapse as you breathe in and out. Notice your stomach lift and subside with each breath.

'Observe the gap between breathing in and breathing out, and breathing out and breathing in. It's called *kumbhaka*. Notice the thought that floats in. Don't fight it or try to suppress it. Notice it. Then bring your attention back to the breath. The thought will float away. Notice the gap between your thoughts.'

She halted again. The family breathed in silence.

Ten minutes later, they opened their eyes.

Dharma Raj: 'Every time I do this, I realise again how important it is to breathe correctly.'

Nachiket: 'Haven't we been doing it all our lives? From the moment we were born? Nobody taught us how to breathe!'

Dharma Raj: 'More's the pity!'

Gargi: 'There's an optimal way of doing everything in life: eating, chewing, walking, sleeping, sitting, standing … why not breathing? It doesn't hurt to do these things correctly. Controlling our breathing could help us pull back from the mental chatter that afflicts most of us.'

Dharma Raj: 'Control is not enough. Breathing patterns get set in infancy. Look carefully at a newborn child. Her stomach moves when she's breathing easily. If she gets upset, it's the chest that moves. That's fearful breathing.'

Gargi: 'Baba, ideal *Pranayamic* breathing engages both the belly and the chest.'

Dharma Raj: 'Of course. I am talking about understanding the link between our body and our emotions. Fear is not a bad thing. Everyone experiences it, and it is useful, a handy instinct. But what if you are in a state of fear all day, for no good reason? What if it's a learned emotional spiral from early childhood?'

Lopamudra: 'Is there an ideal way to breathe?'

Dharma Raj: 'Ideally, two-thirds of your breath should be connected with the belly, the remaining with the chest. Observe your breath, like she said. If there is a lot of chest breathing, ask yourself if you are fearful. If yes, then what is it that you fear? For many of us, that in itself can be a fearful question. We like to believe we don't fear anything!'

Gargi: 'Take baby steps in self-awareness. Do you find yourself breathing in short, stressful bursts when you are running late for work? Kit, does your breathing lack rhythm when you are arguing with me? I know mine does! Do we lose the rhythm when we are around people we dislike? Or resent?'

Nachiket: 'Notice your breathing. Hmmm ... I suppose the least we can do is take three deep breaths in silence, three times a day, maybe. That would at least bring us back to the present moment.'

Dharma Raj: 'The present moment, that's the important thing. Breathing is the only thing in the present moment that we can consciously control. Everything else ... thoughts, feelings, plans ... they can all exist in the past or the future, as well as in the present. We cannot save our breath for the future. We cannot use breaths taken in the past to keep us afloat today. Breathing is only in the present. So, if we focus our mind on breathing, we are, in effect, also focusing on the present.'

Nachiket: 'Garu, can the breath be divided into distinct elements?'

Gargi: 'Yes. *Puraka* is inhalation. Slow and deep, using the diaphragm. *Antarkumbhaka* is retaining the air from the inhaled breath. *Rechaka* is exhaling, which must also be slow. And finally, *Bahya Kumbhaka* is the pause after the exhalation and before the next inhalation. At this stage, the lungs are empty. The muscles should stay relaxed when you begin the next cycle.'

Dharma Raj: 'The aim of *Pranayama* is to achieve moments of thoughtlessness. When seized by thoughts, the breathing rate and the heart rate increase. When the thought process slows down, the breathing and heart rate slow down too. Interestingly, the respiratory, circulatory and wakefulness centres in our body are in close physical proximity to the medulla oblongata in the brain stem. When you slow down your breathing, you soothe the nervous system.'

Gargi: 'Deepak Chopra says that *Pranayama* balances the right and left hemispheres of the brain—the intuitive and logical halves.'

Lopamudra: 'I got up early for a *Pranayama* session, but I can see this has become a discussion—as usual! Let's at least do the *Nadi Shodhana*, Garu.'

Gargi: 'Okay. A few words first, Aai.' She turned her head to look at her husband. 'It's a breathing exercise that's meant to balance our biochemistry.'

She began her demonstration, even as she continued speaking. 'First, fold the index and middle finger into the palm of your right hand. Take a deep breath. Press the right nostril with your thumb and breathe out from your left nostril. Pause. Take a long breath in from your left nostril. Pause as you press the left nostril with your ring and little finger and release your right nostril. Breathe out slowly, observing your breath the whole time. Pause. Take a deep breath in from the same side. Pause as you press the right nostril with your thumb and release your left nostril. Breathe out. This completes one count.'

Nachiket: 'Okay.'

Gargi: 'You'll notice that it's easier to breathe from one nostril than the other, or that the breath you release is cool on one side and warm on the other. Gradually, these imbalances are corrected.'

Lopamudra: 'Let's begin. We'll do nine counts.'

The family finished the exercise and sat in silence. Then Nachiket said, 'We should be leaving.'

Lopamudra: 'Another cup of tea before you leave?'

Gargi: 'No, Aai. Thanks. I must get back in time for the class. And Kit must get to work. But we'll meet soon.'

Dharma Raj: 'Next time, bring Anirban too. Is he interested in spiritual matters as well?'

Nachiket: 'Not at all! But he's spirited. And he knows a lot. He travels a lot. He's a rationalist.'

Gargi: 'Whatever that means. What are we then? Irrationalists?'

Dharma Raj laughed. 'May both the tribes increase! We can always try and expand the horizons of his rationality.'

Nachiket: 'How?'

Dharma Raj: 'I am sure we can think of something. Maybe we could talk about subjects that most rationalists are wary of? Like God? Deities? Idol worship!'

Gargi: 'Cheers to that! Let's go, Kit.'

Gargi picked up Nachiket's bag, while he reached for their helmets. Dharma Raj and Lopamudra watched as the young couple headed off towards their bike, and to another day filled with promise.

AFTERWORD

The Kauravas have their strengths. The Pandavas have their weaknesses. The Kauravas have their virtues. The Pandavas have their vices. That being said, it would not have felt right if the Kauravas had won the Great War. Why?

Lord Ram has his moments of hesitation. Lady Sita has intensity. Guru Vashishtha and Guru Vishwamitra have their mutual antagonism. Raavan is all hurt; Kumbhakarna is all heart. Manthara has her pain ... How do we judge?

Lord Shiva has anger. Lady Kali has her grouse. Lord Ganesh has his secrets and Parvateshwar has his limits. Brahaspati has his self-satisfaction. And Lady Sati, her self-imposed chains. Whom do we emulate? To what extent?

The Pandavas engage with their failings and try to rise above them. They use self-scrutiny. Sure, they make mistakes, and frequently fail their better selves. But their diligence makes them learn from their mistakes.

The Kauravas are unable to be witness to their own acts. This is their biggest failing. They blame others, they question their circumstances. They are unable to take responsibility for their misfortunes and actions. Their negligence gradually makes their worst tendencies overpower their better qualities.

Lord Ram lives in a constant state of self-scrutiny. So does Kumbhakarna. *Diligence.*

Manthara sees hostility and machinations everywhere, not much else. And Raavan is caught in a whirlpool of egotistic desires and torture. Masochism and its inverted hell—sadism. *Negligence.*

Lord Shiva relentlessly strives to understand, win over, and do what must be done. Even his anger is put to work. He knows no rest. Lord Ganesh is in a state of constant self-regulation and protectiveness towards others. Lady Sati painstakingly undoes her chains. *Diligence.*

Lady Kali's anger arrests her softening. Parvateshwar trims his mind's searching questions. Brahaspati's mind clouds the messages from his heart. *Negligence.*

Perhaps these two words are the key takeaways from these stories: Diligence. कर्मठ. Negligence. लापरवाही.

Negligence makes us behave unintendedly. It leads to action without awareness. It is habitual, unexamined, inattentive. It looks for excuses and finds them with ease. Indignation, outrage and judgement towards others are its weapons.

Negligence has some favourite phrases: 'I forgot.' 'I didn't mean it.' 'It didn't strike me.' 'That's not fair.' 'It was his fault.' 'She should not have done that.' 'Why me?' 'I was helpless.' 'I deserve better.' 'I will not do it next time, I promise.' 'I will do it tomorrow ... next month ... next year ...' 'But why can't you/she/he do it?'

Negligent people may have their moments of honesty and genuine remorse. For some, these are pivotal moments, and the negligence fades away. For others, they are the endpoints. They do not carry forward. There is no subsequent behavioural change. Over time, such a person devolves through sheer inertia, distraction and absence of will power.

Diligence embraces action, effort, efficiency, discipline. It welcomes change. It fights the small battles. Like waking up at six in the morning. Today, tomorrow, every day. Diligence understands responsibility and shuns excuses. It does not count on the diligence of others. It seeks rhythm. It shuns fantasy and escapist dreams. Its weapons are imagination, focus, self-scrutiny. It prefers example over advice to influence others. It influences others best when it does not seek to influence others. It does not impose.

They are within us, all of them—Lord Shiva, Lady Sati, Parvateshwar, Lady Kali, Lord Ganesh, Brahaspati, Lord Ram, Lady Sita, Raavan, Kumbhakarna, Manthara, Duryodhana, Drona, Bhishma, Yudhishtra, Bhima, Kunti, Gandhari, Dhritarashtra, Abhimanyu, Draupadi, Dushasana…

And, of course, all of us are Arjuna in our potential. But Arjuna must stop in his tracks and acknowledge his confusion before he can engage in battle. Confusion is good as a stepping-stone, it can inspire seeking and learning. Too many certainties about life and oneself can lead to an unexamined life that fails to rise to its potential.

When the disciple in us is ready, the Master within—our inner Lord Krishna—will appear, to guide us on the path towards wisdom. And a truly purposeful life.

SELECT BIBLIOGRAPHY

B.N. Patnaik, 'The Killing of Dussasana', *SaralaMahabharat. blogspot.com*, http://saralamahabharat.blogspot.com/2008/04/killing-of-dussasana.html, 3 April 2008.

'Breathing Guide', *Saagara*, http://www.saagara.com/learning-center/deep-breathing-pranayama-guide.

Deepak Chopra, *Perfect Health*. Random House Australia, Sydney, 2011.

Devdutt Pattanaik, *Jaya*. Penguin Random House, New Delhi, 2010.

Matt Merchant, 'Breathing and Emotions Part II: Fear Pattern Breathing', *YouTube*, https://www.youtube.com/watch?v=VM_jvu2e0ww, 14 November 2012.

Osho, 'The Greatest Miracle In Our Lives', *Speaking Tree*, https://www.speakingtree.inarticle/the-greatest-miracle-in-our-lives, 26 June 2015.

Rajiv Malhotra, *Indra's Net*. HarperCollins Publishers India, New Delhi, 2015.

S.K. Mandal, *Advanced Educational Psychology*. PHI Learning Pvt Ltd, New Delhi, 2002.

Saint Augustine, *Augustine: Confessions and Enchiridion*. Translated and edited by Albert C. Outler. Westminster Press, 1955.

St Paul's Epistle to the Romans, New Testament Ch 7, 15: 25.

Steve Ross with Olivia Rosewood, *Happy Yoga: 7 Reasons Why There's Nothing to Worry About*. HarperCollins Publishers, 2003.

Vinita Bali with Sadhguru, 'The Next Step', *In Conversation with the Mystic*, https://www.youtube.com/watch?v=Bbtywen KTls&ab_channel=Sadhguru, 15 April 2015.

Other Titles by Amish

The Shiva Trilogy

The fastest-selling book series in the history of Indian publishing

THE IMMORTALS OF MELUHA
(Book 1 of the Trilogy)

1900 BC. What modern Indians mistakenly call the Indus Valley Civilisation, the inhabitants of that period knew as the land of Meluha – a near perfect empire created many centuries earlier by Lord Ram. Now their primary river Saraswati is drying, and they face terrorist attacks from their enemies from the east. Will their prophesied hero, the Neelkanth, emerge to destroy evil?

THE SECRET OF THE NAGAS
(Book 2 of the Trilogy)

The sinister Naga warrior has killed his friend Brahaspati and now stalks his wife Sati. Shiva, who is the prophesied destroyer of evil, will not rest till he finds his demonic adversary. His thirst for revenge will lead him to the door of the Nagas, the serpent people. Fierce battles will be fought and unbelievable secrets revealed in the second part of the Shiva trilogy.

THE OATH OF THE VAYUPUTRAS
(Book 3 of the Trilogy)

Shiva reaches the Naga capital, Panchavati, and prepares for a holy war against his true enemy. The Neelkanth must not fail, no matter what the cost. In his desperation, he reaches out to the Vayuputras. Will he succeed? And what will be the real cost of battling Evil? Read the concluding part of this bestselling series to find out.

The Ram Chandra Series

The second fastest-selling book series in the history of Indian publishing

RAM – SCION OF IKSHVAKU
(Book 1 of the Series)

He loves his country and he stands alone for the law. His band of brothers, his wife, Sita and the fight against the darkness of chaos. He is Prince Ram. Will he rise above the taint that others heap on him? Will his love for Sita sustain him through his struggle? Will he defeat the demon Raavan who destroyed his childhood? Will he fulfil the destiny of the Vishnu? Begin an epic journey with Amish's latest the Ram Chandra Series.

SITA – WARRIOR OF MITHILA
(Book 2 of the Series)

An abandoned baby is found in a field. She is adopted by the ruler of Mithila, a powerless kingdom, ignored by all. Nobody believes this child will amount to much. But they are wrong. For she is no ordinary girl. She is Sita. Through an innovative multi-linear narrative, Amish takes you deeper into the epic world of the Ram Chandra Series.

RAAVAN – ENEMY OF ARYAVARTA
(Book 3 of the Series)

Raavan is determined to be a giant among men, to conquer, plunder, and seize the greatness that he thinks is his right. He is a man of contrasts, of brutal violence and scholarly knowledge. A man who will love without reward and kill without remorse. In this, the third book in the Ram Chandra series, Amish sheds light on Raavan, the king of Lanka. Is he the greatest villain in history or just a man in a dark place, all the time?

WAR OF LANKA
(Book 4 of the Series)

Sita has been kidnapped. Defiantly, she dares Raavan to kill her - she'd rather die than allow Ram to surrender. Ram is beside himself with grief and rage. He prepares for war. Fury is his fuel. Calm focus, his guide. Raavan thought he was invincible. He thought he'd negotiate and force a surrender. Little did he know ...

The first three books of the second-fastest-selling book series in Indian publishing history - the Ram Chandra Series – explore the individual journeys of Ram, Sita and Raavan. In this, the epic fourth book of the series, their narrative strands crash into each other, and explode in a slaughterous war.

Indic Chronicles

LEGEND OF SUHELDEV

Repeated attacks by Mahmud of Ghazni have weakened India's northern regions. Then the Turks raid and destroy one of the holiest temples in the land: the magnificent Lord Shiva temple at Somnath. At this most desperate of times, a warrior rises to defend the nation. King Suheldev—fierce rebel, charismatic leader, inclusive patriot. Read this epic adventure of courage and heroism that recounts the story of that lionhearted warrior and the magnificent Battle of Bahraich.

Non-fiction

IMMORTAL INDIA

Explore India with the country's storyteller, Amish, who helps you understand it like never before, through a series of sharp articles, nuanced speeches and intelligent debates. In *Immortal India*, Amish lays out the vast landscape of an ancient culture with a fascinatingly modern outlook.

30 Years *of*

 HarperCollins *Publishers* India

At HarperCollins, we believe in telling the best stories and finding the widest possible readership for our books in every format possible. We started publishing 30 years ago; a great deal has changed since then, but what has remained constant is the passion with which our authors write their books, the love with which readers receive them, and the sheer joy and excitement that we as publishers feel in being a part of the publishing process.

Over the years, we've had the pleasure of publishing some of the finest writing from the subcontinent and around the world, and some of the biggest bestsellers in India's publishing history. Our books and authors have won a phenomenal range of awards, and we ourselves have been named Publisher of the Year the greatest number of times. But nothing has meant more to us than the fact that millions of people have read the books we published, and somewhere, a book of ours might have made a difference.

As we step into our fourth decade, we go back to that one word – a word which has been a driving force for us all these years.

Read.

Harper
Collins

HARPER
PERENNIAL

HARPER
BUSINESS

HARPER
BLACK

हार्पर
हिन्दी

HarperCollins
Children's Books

HARPER
DESIGN

HARPER
VANTAGE

Harper
Sport

Printed by Libri Plureos GmbH in Hamburg, Germany